# Introductions in Feminist Theology

# 10

Editorial Committee

Mary Grey
Lisa Isherwood
Janet Wootton

## Sheffield Academic Press
*A Continuum imprint*

# Introducing Feminist Ecclesiology

Natalie K. Watson

Copyright © 2002 Sheffield Academic Press
*A Continuum imprint*

Published by Sheffield Academic Press Ltd
The Tower Building, 11 York Road, London SE1 7NX
370 Lexington Avenue, New York NY 10017-6550

www.SheffieldAcademicPress.com
www.continuumbooks.com

British Library Cataloguing-in-Publication Data
A catalogue record for this book is available from the British Library

Typeset by Sheffield Academic Press
Printed                              in Great Britain by MPG Books Ltd, Bodmin, Cornwall

ISBN 0-8264-6254-5

# Table of Contents

# Editors' Preface

This is the tenth book in the Introductions in Feminist Theology series and the editors are particularly grateful to Dr Natalie Watson for writing it. For, in fact, it takes great courage to write about ecclesiology from a feminist standpoint, the Church being many women's focal point for both the pain of exclusion from ordained ministry and for the persistent misogyny and devaluing of women within ecclesial life. Indeed, many feminist theologians have shied away from the task, viewing it as inconsistent with feminist integrity. This book does not avoid difficult issues but faces them head-on. 'Why bother with ecclesiology?' the author has been frequently asked, in the context of the continuing exodus from the Church of many women, forced to seek spiritual nourishment elsewhere. 'Because women are Church and always have been' is her response, and the book is a brave attempt to take us beyond the dilemma 'to go or to stay'.

What Natalie Watson presents us with here is a challenging constructive feminist ecclesiology, which 'means writing women as church into the process of theological reflection on the nature and role of the church' (p. 11). Tackling the ambiguous, alienating legacy of history she then shows clearly how key metaphors of Church (such as Bride, Servant, Body of Christ) work in an androcentric excluding way for women, serving to reinforce subordinate roles for women in society. She lets her readers see the significance of the different forms of Women-Church that have arisen in the last 20 years as providing vital space for the formation of alternative ecclesial discourses. These are discourses that honour women's embodied experience and personhood—but at the same time call for a revisioning of the (gender-blind) sacramental experience of the Church as a whole.

The creative contribution that the book offers—both to the series and to theological discourse itself—is the way Natalie Watson develops a narrative ecclesiology that is prophetic, mystical and expresses a sacramental poetics. Along with unity, holiness, catholicity and apostolicity—the traditional four marks of the church—she calls for justice to become recognized as a fifth mark, stressing the link between bodiliness, sacramental experience and actual flourishing in the world. The book draws on insights from Christian feminist theologians and feminist theorists, but certainly makes its own creative contribution. Its strength is the way the understanding of Church is widened from its narrow institutional definition into becoming an active event, where sacraments are experienced as embodied interaction between the individual and the Divine within community. Its specifically feminist character lies in this embodied interaction including 'the diversity of women's bodies as the Body of Christ'.

I welcome this book as a stimulating addition to the series: but, more profoundly, as offering great hope to the many disillusioned people, women and men, who want to look to the church as *lumen gentium* (light of the nations), but who find the burden of the scandal-fraught present overwhelming. There is still a vision to pursue, another story to be told.

Mary Grey
April 2002

# Acknowledgments

No book is ever the work of the author alone and essentially remains work in progress, something I continue to grapple with, as I write and work as a theologian and teacher of theology and church history. I would therefore like to thank those who have shared the journey of writing this book with me.

It had its beginnings as a doctoral thesis at the University of Durham. Professor Ann Loades was an able and constructive midwife to my own thoughts and ideas. It was completed during a painful time in my own life which, however, also became an experience of the love and shared faith of the women and men around me. I would like to thank my friends from many parts of my life and my colleagues and students at Ripon College Cuddesdon for their support and encouragement throughout the completion of this work. Without what I have learnt from them and from the stories they shared with me, this book would not have been the same. Particular thanks to Yvonne Parrey, Melanie and Emily Hall, Jackie Johnson, Karen Gresham, Hugh Jaeger, Graham Woolfenden, Hans-Joachim Kühnle and Claire Henderson Davis. Thanks also to Catherine Norris, Lisa Isherwood, Mary Grey and Janet Wootton for their perceptive editorial comments and for asking me to contribute to this series.

My parents and grandparents have always believed in me and have encouraged me all the way. This book is dedicated to the memory of Daniel F. Kröger, who did not live to see its completion, but would have been excited by it. He sparked off many of the ideas over endless (no doubt sacramental) cups of tea.

# Chapter One

# Methodological Considerations:
# Towards a Framework of Ecclesiological Discourse

This is not another book about 'women *in* the church' or even 'women *and* the church'. A number of these have appeared over the years. The problem with titles such as 'women *in* the church' or 'women *and* the church' is that somehow they make it look as if women and the church are two separate entities or as if women are something with which, or even a group of people with whom, the church has to deal as one of those challenges it has to face at the beginning of a new millennium; something along the lines of 'the church and war' or 'the church and democracy'. Or even the 'Decade of Churches in Solidarity with Women'. This, however, is not what this book is about.

*Women are church and have always been church* (Fiorenza 1982). Therefore they have a say in what the church is, about its life and about how we speak about it in theological terms. We need to reconsider the traditional models of how the church has spoken about itself in the context of patriarchal theologies in the light of this basic premise. The history of the church needs to be reread and rewritten 'on women's terms'. We need to think about the story of the church as the story of the community of women, men and children who grapple with the story of God and seek to tell it through their lives. This leads to an examination of how women themselves have approached the formation of new communities in which 'being church' takes place in a way that is meaningful for them. The ordination of women in some churches of the Reformation, the continuing refusal of the Roman Catholic hierarchy to do so, and the presence of those groups who reject the ordination of women in those churches which have accepted it, point to a discussion of new and different models of ministry. The body, and body theology, have been important in feminist theological reconsiderations and continue to be so (Isherwood and Stuart 1998). Throughout its history the church has maintained the importance of proclaiming the incarnation not only through the spoken word but through embodied acts of celebration, called sacraments. Sacraments and ministry have not been unproblematic for women as they have been excluded from full participation in them and their theological significance has often been based on an inherently misogynistic theological paradigm. Sacraments do, however, convey the message of the incarnation in a way that is too important for women to ignore and therefore a reconsideration of sacramental theology is vital for a feminist rethinking of what it means to be church.

That women are church does not mean women are the church and men are not. Women are church as equal and yet different citizens of the body of Christ. In naming their own experiences, women acknowledge their power and their being in the image of God. By naming themselves as those who are church, women claim their power to name the church as the space where such naming of their own experiences and of the Triune God as being-in-life-giving-relation can take place. Feminist ecclesiology is one way among others for women to speak about their being church and their embodying the divine in the world.

Before I begin to discuss and evaluate the situation of feminist ecclesiology, it is necessary to outline a theological framework, a starting point from which such an evaluation can take place. What does it mean for women to rethink what it means to be church? Where do we start and what are we aiming for?

The starting point is one of fundamental ambivalence. It is possible to read the history of the church as one of women's suffering, of an institution that has gone out of its way to exclude, to marginalize, to oppress women often purely on the grounds of their being women. From the earliest days of the Christian Church, the development of hierarchical and clerical structures has run in parallel with the increasing marginalization and oppression of women and their discourses of faith. Women have been excluded from most of the churches' meaningful moments. Those churches which understand them-selves as churches of 'the Word' often do not permit women to preach. Churches that put high emphasis on the sacraments have banned women from the sanctuary on the grounds of their supposed ritual impurity—or indeed merely on the grounds that Christ, the source of the Christian priesthood, happened to be incarnate as a male human being—and reduced them to mere recipients of some sacraments while they are entirely excluded from others. The church has been, and continues to be, a place where women suffer institutional injustice, where women are told of their supposed in-significance, where a theology of womanhood is preached that defines a meaningful life for women either in terms of childbirth or in terms of the rejection of their sexuality. Even though the present Pope speaks about the supposed 'dignity' of women, his concept of 'dignity' defines women's lives solely in terms of their relationship with men. Thereby it excludes a large number of women who do not define themselves in terms of heterosexual marriage and childbirth. He goes as far as challenging victims of rape at the hand of Serb soldiers to give birth to and love the children from pregnancies which are the results of that mass rape.

In the light of such a dark picture, the question that comes to mind is: why bother with the church? Why do not women in large numbers follow the example of Mary Daly's 'exodus' out of the patriarchal church into a new and feminist future? Mary Daly, a distinguished scholar, holding three doctorates, was the first woman to be allowed to preach at Harvard Memorial Chapel. She used this occasion to perform a symbolic exodus in which she asked women, men and children to follow her out of the church, an institution which was irredeemably patriarchal and which symbolized the oppression of women and patriarchal religion itself in its most archetypal form.

So, why bother indeed? Feminist and other scholars have unearthed a different picture of the church too. The church, though excluding women from some of its most meaningful moments, has also been the space in which women have been able to develop their own discourses of faith, often against or in spite of patriarchy. The religious life provided women with a unique space in which to develop a 'women's world' in which men were often simply accepted visitors. The movement for women's suffrage at the beginning of the twentieth century was carried by Christian concerns. Though refused the opportunity to minister at home, women missionaries have often pioneered Christianity in other parts of the world. More generally, women account for the majority of those who attend church services. In fact, an Irish Roman Catholic priest, who was opposed to the ordination of women, once told me that he thought that God had designed the priesthood to be male to ensure that at least some men went to church. So, women are involved in the life of the church and continue to be in large numbers. A long list of examples could be given and a movement of rewriting the history of the church as her-story is beginning to take shape. The church has, as well as being a space of oppression, been a space which has in the past—and continues in the present—to create meaning for women. In many ways, it is a 'given' that has to be part of the agenda if the task of feminist theology is the rethinking and rewriting of Christian theology in a paradigm that acknowledges women's being church, celebrates it and regards any understanding that does not recognize women as church as incomplete.

The challenge for women at the onset of the third millennium of the existence of the Christian Church is to find ways of living and working with this fundamental ambivalence. For some women the experience of oppression, having their concerns/rights rendered trivial or being forced to assume a male perspective in worship, preaching and doing theology, has become unbearable. Some women, post-Christian feminist thinkers such as Mary Daly and Daphne Hampson among the most prominent, have left the church behind as an institution which no longer creates meaning for them. Others continue to persevere and to work towards transformation from within. They refuse to leave the church, to leave Christianity to those who see their own patriarchal framework of thought as the only possible one and work in terms of constructive resistance from within. Often these women experience their own lives as those of 'resident aliens'. Yet, the starting point for a feminist reconsideration of what it means to be church cannot be the question of an either/or: is the church an irredeemably patriarchal institution which women have to leave behind if they want to lead meaningful spiritual lives or is it possible to work from within and discover the liberating potential the church might still hold? The starting point for a feminist reconsideration of ecclesiology is that of learning to live with ambivalence, to somehow make sense of the reality of oppression and empowerment, of liberation and suffering, of silence and powerful speech at the same time. A feminist rethinking of what it means to be church has to take into account both positions, the many different reasons why women stay and the equally numerous and persuasive reasons why women leave or remain on the margins of the church. The question a feminist ecclesiology has to answer is not whether or not women ought to 'leave' or 'stay', but how it is possible to rethink what it means to be church within a theological paradigm which aims at reconsidering the basics of Christian theology and practice in feminist terms.

A number of other questions have to be asked before I can set out on this project. The title of this book is *Introducing Feminist Ecclesiology*. Ecclesiology, however, is not a term which feminist scholars have used widely and it carries as much baggage as the church itself. So, one necessary question is: what is ecclesiology? and why are we doing it? Why not just talk about the church? Ecclesiology as a theological discipline was born out of a historical need, a situation which made it necessary for the church to define itself. One of those situations which made it necessary to work out what it means to be the church was the Donatist crisis in the fourth century. A group of North African Christians claimed to be the pure church which had survived the persecution without surrendering the Holy Scriptures to the authorities of the Roman Empire. Yet, more importantly, they proclaimed that those who had surrendered and denied the Christian faith under torture no longer had the right to consider themselves part of the body of Christ. For most of the history of the church, however, women have not so much been denied their being church due to supposed impurity on the grounds of what they have *done*, but for fear of defilement due to *what they are*. The Donatist crisis was eventually resolved both through the interference of imperial power structures and through Augustine of Hippo's argument that the church is a 'mixed body', a space where saints and sinners, tares and wheat, exist together. It is the experience of many women today that they are 'accepted' in the church though regarded as 'tares' which defile and destroy the purity of the wheat. Yet, all over the world, women are claiming their power of naming the church and naming themselves, not as tares in the wheat, but rather as life-giving 'leaven in the lump'. This is essentially a breaking of unhealthy dualisms. It is claiming the right to question the concept of defining some individuals as saints and others as sinners. And it goes further: it challenges the very structures that define saintliness and sinfulness. Yet it is not only about the church as an institution, but about the people, women, men and children, who are the church of a God whose very being is in life-giving and life-sustaining relation.

Ecclesiology has come a long way since the fourth century. Where does feminist ecclesiology enter the discussion and what is it trying to achieve? First of all, feminist ecclesiology is responding to a situation of profound ambiguity. In writing formal ecclesiology from a feminist perspective, I am entering a conversation to which I have not been invited. Surveying the mainstream ecclesiological literature, I cannot think of many major books written by women. As an analysis of recent ecclesiological writings by Roman Catholic and Reformed theologians shows, ecclesiology has been written by men and for men. Looking at Women's Studies Departments in institutions of higher education and more general feminist literature, those who bother with religion, let alone in its institutionalized form, are few and far between. A poster advertising a lecture I gave at the Women's Studies Department of an Australian university had to have a footnote, defining the word 'ecclesiology', anticipating that scholars of secular feminism would not even know what it was. Many women are leaving the church and seeking their spirituality outside the church or on its margins. Voices like this one are heard more and more often:

> Women and religion are at a crossroads. If women are not taken seriously and their talents recognized, I think there will be serious consequences. I've had three daughters and they are *not* drawn to current religious traditions. They see no place for women. They see women within the Roman tradition differing significantly on matters of human sexuality and issues affecting women. Why join such confusion? (Winter *et al.* 1994: 12).

A growing number of women see the institutional frameworks of traditional denominations no longer as the focus of their spiritual lives:

> I think my spiritual identity is moving away from the church, largely because the church seems preoccupied over who 'owns' it, or who is 'in' or 'out' and why. I find that activity life-destroying and the God of that activity demonic, a God I do not 'worship', let alone desire to serve (Winter *et al.* 1994: 41).

And yet, women are church and have always been church. Though women have, to a large extent, not been involved in formal ecclesiological dialogues, such as the debates of the Second Vatican Council, this does not mean that women have not participated in the life of the church and that they have not reflected on their presence within it. Feminist ecclesiology therefore needs to take account of women's presence and to analyse the significance of women for the development of the ecclesiological debate.

If the church is perceived as a 'given' and as a cultural religious institution of value for women and men, this points to the necessity of a more formal, critical and constructive reflection on what the church is. We need to discover both traditional and new ways of expressing what church is. These need to be relevant to both women and men and outline the church as a context in which the lives of women, men and children take place. The importance of the church as the space for discourses of faith, sacramental celebration and community urges the necessity of not discarding ecclesiology altogether, but of rethinking discourses of being church. Ecclesiology can be understood as a form of male discourse by which men have attempted to define valid and invalid forms of being church as well as identifying women's discourses of church as not being church (Jantzen 1996). Grace Jantzen suggests, following Luce Irigaray and Foucault, the necessity of reassessing the function of religion as one of the most important factors in culture, disrupting discourses that have in the past been defined almost exclusively by men. I want to question the function of ecclesiology as a discourse that describes the church as a vital religious space, but does so in a way that supports a particular, predominantly patriarchal social symbolic order. The subject matter of ecclesiology is, from a critical feminist point of view, the church or its theological essence as a means of legitimizing and sanctioning an ordering of society which leaves no space for women's discourses of faith (Ruether 1985). A feminist reconsideration of ecclesiology is therefore an act of reclaiming an area of theology and the life of the church that in the past has been largely a male domain. Thinking about the church in theological terms has been a central part of being church throughout its history. It is time for women to participate in it on their own terms.

A useful starting point might be revisiting the location in which traditional systematic theology has placed theological reflections on the church. Ecclesiology has its traditional place between theological anthropology and eschatology, between theological considerations on what it means to be human in the image of God and on the 'last things', theological reflections on the state of this world in the light of the *parousia*, the second coming of Christ, the end of the world and the last judgment. It has been important for feminist theological scholars to think about both aspects and to situate their theological reflections at the intersection of those two discourses. The question of what it means for women to be human, of sexual particularity and difference, of different relationships, of the body, are essential prerequisites for speaking theologically about women's being church. Feminist theologians have also worked on rethinking the concept of theological eschatology. Eschatology can no longer mean a theological discourse which deals with the next world, with the transcendent. Feminist theological eschatology is a theological reflection on the situation of *this* world. The situation of this world has to be evaluated in terms of the need for an awareness of the essential interconnectedness of the human and the non-human creation and in terms of justice. Mary Grey makes this connection and urges a dialogue between theological reflections on the church and the concerns of ecofeminist theologians (Grey 1997a). Women cannot be contented with simply being assured that they are part of the church as a spiritual body; their presence and participation has to be expressed in the very structures in which the church as the embodiment of the Triune God manifests itself here and now.

Feminist ecclesiology has to make the connection between what it means to be human and what it means to live in this world as it is today. As such it involves a necessary re-evaluation of the prophetic presence in this world as well as a reconsideration of what it means for the church to be at the intersection between this world and the transcendent, between the human and non-human creation and the divine. It is at this intersection that discourses of justice and liberation can and do take place, and being church can begin to mean being an open community of liberated human bodies who celebrate their own lives in the image of, and essentially as part of, the life of the Triune God in this world.

The next question that arises is: who are women? I have already pointed out that women, though they represent a large proportion of those who attend church services and work within the church, take a wide variety of different standpoints as to what meaning this institution which they, be it faithfully or within a love/hate relationship, support or have left behind. That process of leaving behind is often a painful process of bereavement and at the same time an important part of their identity as liberated women of faith. Early discourses in feminist theology have often been criticized as speaking for all women from a white-educated middle-class North American point of view, without taking into account the voices and concerns of those women who do not belong to this group. It is therefore important to work from the assumption that feminist ecclesiology does not attempt to speak on behalf of anyone, be it in general terms, or in particular. It is the task of a feminist ecclesiology to develop criteria through which it is possible to assess both traditional and new ways of being church and determine whether they take account of the lives and the presence of women as church. This involves most fundamentally an openness for diversity: is the church as it is described in theological terms a space in which women can be who they are, in which there is room for their bodies, for their different sexualities and sexual orientations? Do different ecclesiologies speak about women being church, whoever and wherever they are, as lesbians, as women in heterosexual or non-sexual relationships? Does ecclesiology as speaking of the church in theological terms ask women to assume the role of the generic male reader or does it speak about the church in terms which are meaningful for women and enable women to celebrate their being women within the body of Christ?

Another question, which the task of doing ecclesiology within a framework of feminist theology raises, is: which church are we talking about? This is one of the key challenges of doing ecclesiology in the present situation. The church, as ecclesiology discusses it, is both a spiritual entity, something which Christians believe to be 'one, holy, catholic and apostolic', and an institution, a political body which is divided into 'denominations'. Denominations are particular historical and political manifestations of church in particular historical, cultural, social and political contexts. Ecclesiology somehow has to speak about both. This provides us with what is essentially another situation of ambiguity. The writing of ecclesiology takes place within a particular political situation, usually that of a particular denomination. This, however, is a volume within an introductory series introducing a number of different topics within feminist theology. It does not set a particular denominational context. Events such as the First European Women's Synod in Gmunden, Austria in 1996, the WISE (Wales, Ireland, Scotland and England) Women's Synod in Liverpool in 1999 or the history of the Women-Church movement in North America, which will be discussed in more detail later in this book, show that for some women being church takes place in a particular institutional or denominational context, while, for others, small independent communities which celebrate experimental women's liturgies and work for causes of social justice are the prime locations of their spiritual lives. My discussion of women's being church essentially has to take account of both and attempt to establish a constructive dialogue between them. Feminist ecclesiology takes place, like all feminist liberation theologies, in the constructive tension between being essentially contextual and at the same time celebrating the *diversity of contexts* in which it occurs. My own writing of feminist ecclesiology is very much shaped by the discovery of the catholic and Anglican context into which I have grown as I was working on the subject. At the same time it has been nurtured by the dialogue with women from a variety of other contexts such as the life of Free Churches, Congregationalist and Baptist Churches and other traditions within the Church of England to which I belong.

Feminist theology is essentially transgressive and subversive theology. By this I do not only mean the important role which women have played in the development of the ecumenical movement in this century. Women have often been the pioneers of ecumenical dialogue on a local basis long before official ecumenical debates and negotiations caught up with what was already going on through personal relationships and small groups. Feminist theology crosses boundaries which have been set by patriarchy. One of these boundaries/ limitations is the thinking about the church in merely institutional terms. Rosemary Radford Ruether, one of the pioneers of feminist ecclesiology, has criticized the church for its exclusive focus on its institutional nature. The task of a feminist ecclesiology is twofold: it does involve thinking and speaking theologically about the church as an institution and about the particular institutions in which the church exists, but it goes beyond this focus on the institutions in discussing a variety of different models by which the church describes itself in theological terms. It has to be asked whether these models proposed by theologians working within a patriarchal framework are sufficient for describing women's being church. Closer examination reveals that this is not the case as women are often excluded from the centres of institutional and defining power within these frameworks. In addition, many of these frameworks operate with gender-power constructions which assume a subordinate role for women or ignore women's existence altogether. Feminist ecclesiology rephrases the questions asked. The question cannot merely be: *what* is the church? but *who* is the church? Some women have moved from one denomination to another because they were able to find space for their vocation to the ordained ministry to be validated by the church. Some women have left the Roman Catholic Church in order to pursue their vocation to the ministerial priesthood in the Anglican or Methodist Church, which they were denied by the institutional Roman Catholic Church. Others left the Church of England prior to the vote for the ordination of women in 1992 and emigrated to the United States or Australia where Anglican churches such as the Episcopal Church were already ordaining women. Groups such as the Metropolitan Community Church were founded in order to create a space for those excluded from the worship and life of other denominations, particularly gay and lesbian people. Yet this book is not about evaluating whether one particular institution or denomination is a better place for women than another. The kind of feminist ecclesiological discourse which I propose seeks to provide criteria by which ecclesiological discourses of a variety of different theological, ecclesial and political contexts can be evaluated. They should be means by which it is possible to discern whether particular ecclesiological discourses describe ways of being church, in terms of theological discourse and women's ecclesial practice, which take into account women's being church and see them as a meaningful resource for the church's theological self-understanding.

It is important to rethink the significance of boundaries in which ecclesiological discourses take place. By this I mean particularly boundaries of traditions and of existing disciplines. Feminist ecclesiology has to take place both on the brink and within the existing boundaries. Women's discourses of faith and theology have to identify the boundaries largely set and defined by men and seek to transcend them. Most feminist theological discourses so far have largely been confined to the theology and the church of the Christian West. I propose to focus more feminist theological attention on the various Orthodox traditions, both in terms of analysing the role and the experiences of women within the churches of the Christian East and in terms of evaluating Orthodox conceptions of being church alongside Roman Catholic and Protestant ones. This is particularly important with regard to the importance of the Trinity for Orthodox ecclesiology as a vital complement to a sacramental and incarnational feminist ecclesiology. So feminist theologians need to transcend male-made boundaries, but on the other hand recognize them as frameworks which have created meaning for women and their discourses of faith.

The other set of boundaries that require critical evaluation are those of theological and academic disciplines. The fact that the term 'ecclesiology' is rarely used by feminist theologians suggests that feminist theological discourse is by its nature interdisciplinary. A feminist reconsideration of ecclesiology needs not only to be in dialogue with other theological *topoi* such as Christology, theological anthropology and the doctrine of the Trinity, but needs to draw on subjects such as practical theology, church history, sociology of religion, religious studies and women's studies. Feminist ecclesiology recognizes the ambiguity of male-defined boundaries for women and their discourses of faith, theology and spirituality, transcends them and also seeks to find ways of working constructively within them.

Feminist ecclesiology means writing women as church into the process of theological reflection on the nature and the role of the church. This debate takes place both within the church and in an academic context. Recent sociological studies have shown that many women seek their spirituality outside the church, rather than within it. Yet the church remains an important social institution which has created and continues to create meaning for women and yet is largely defined by men. That, however, does not mean that women have not reflected on the church and their being in it, be it in terms of alienation, belonging or reconsideration. Feminist ecclesiology takes place in a double dialogue with both traditional male-defined ecclesiologies and feminist discussions of the church. Both of these have to be analysed using the means of a feminist reader-response method. Do existing ecclesiological discourses take account of women, their lives and their bodies and do they write women's lives and women's bodies into the body of Christ? Here, for example, a critical analysis of the use of liberation theology and the idea of base ecclesial communities by feminist theologians of the 1980s is necessary. Feminist ecclesiology works with multiple resources. Traditional ecclesiological documents such as those of the Second Vatican Council are only one group of resources; the experiences and the praxis of women's networks within and across the boundaries of traditional denominations, such as the Catholic Women's Network or the Women-Church movements in North America and in Australia, or the Women's Synod movement in Europe, are another.

Feminist ecclesiology is feminist in that it takes account of women's lives— of women's experiences of faith and sexuality—as a vital source for the reconsideration of ecclesiology. In its analysis of existing material it needs to identify the construction of gender-power constructs through ecclesiology and the models and metaphors it uses. It then needs to advocate sexual difference and ultimately a multiplicity of different identities which participate in and embody the body of Christ. Feminist ecclesiology uses the methods of feminist theory and feminist theological hermeneutics in providing a critical analysis of the theological self-understanding and the ecclesial praxis of Christian Churches. It aims at a creative and constructive rewriting of ecclesiology in order to enable multiple discourses of being church. In doing that, its audience is twofold: it creates theological means with which women can evaluate and describe the institutional and para-institutional ways in which their being church takes place, and it contributes to the wider debate about what it means to be the Christian Church at the beginning of the third millennium of its existence.

So, how do we go about it? The chapter following these initial methodological reflections which set the framework for what follows will look in more detail at the ambivalent legacy of history. A short survey of the history of the church will show how the work of reconsidering ecclesiology is the task both of a historian and a theologian. The aim of this brief historical survey is not to seek justification from the past for transforming the church of the present and the future, but to understand women's reconsiderations of ecclesiology as participation in a long history of women as church.

Chapter 3 will discuss and evaluate some of the key models and metaphors which the church has used throughout its history to describe itself. Using hermeneutical tools and methods developed by feminist biblical scholars, I will look at how particular concepts of church have at best left a legacy of ambivalent feelings for women, by on the one hand largely ignoring the presence of women as church and on the other hand creating women's lives by using images of the submissive feminine and heteropatriarchal relationships as its most fundamental structures. What does it mean for women to be part of the 'body of Christ' when their own bodies are rendered impure and excluded from the most significant moments of its life? Can women be part of 'the people of God', which defines itself largely in terms of patriarchal/kyriarchal structures? Can the church be relevant to lesbians and women who do not see heterosexual marriage as a key part of their identities if the relationship between Christ, the male head of the Church, and his bride, the submissive feminine Church, is perceived by some as the fundamental structure of all relationships? I will discuss the ambiguous nature of these core metaphors of ecclesiological discourse and ask whether it is possible to develop an alternative subversive and critical rereading of some of them which might make it possible to redeem them for feminist ecclesiological discourses. Finally, it is also necessary to ask about the possibility of new and different metaphors which regard women's liberation as an essential aspect of being church.

Chapter 4 will look at women's alternative discourses of being church as a vital space in which the feminist ecclesiological debate has taken shape in the last twenty years. Here I will discuss the history and theology of the Women-Church movement in North America and the experiences of women's networks and synods in Europe. What are the theological ideas behind those alternative structures which women have created in order to reclaim their being church? Are they the only possible way for women who seek spirituality within, outside or on the margins of Christianity?

Chapter 5 will discuss ministry as a key moment in the life of the church from which women have largely been excluded throughout the history of most of the Christian Churches. Feminist theologians such as Rosemary Radford Ruether have identified 'clericalism' as one of the destructive factors for women in the patriarchal church. And yet the struggle for the admission of women to the ordained ministry has been one of the most important victories for women in the history of some Christian Churches. The ordained ministry remains an ambivalent topic among feminist scholars. The North American Women-Church movement has partly developed out of the rejection of women's ordination as a key goal, as some women saw it as asking for token participation in the life of a patriarchal church. In this chapter, I ask whether this rejection is the only possible way to go and how a new and transformed theology of ministry can be a key aspect in transforming the life of the church. I will assert that women's being church is much wider than the ordained ministry, but that ordained ministry is a form of participation in the life of the church which is meaningful for those women who feel called to it and can be a means of empowerment for new and transformed structures within the church. The ordination of women can, then, be seen as an important symbol of women's struggle for power and empowerment within the church.

In Chapter 6, I will discuss the possibility of a feminist sacramental ecclesiology as part of an incarnational embodied feminist theology. As well as discussing the idea of sacraments in more general terms, I will look at particular sacraments and their significance for women and consider the question of whether the traditional canon of two, three or seven sacraments has not been a patriarchal restriction that women have had to overcome in order to develop new concepts of the sacramental rooted in women's personhood, women's bodily experiences, interconnectedness and justice for the whole of creation, both human and non-human.

Chapter 7 is entitled 'Beyond "In" or "Out": Reframing the Ecclesiological Debate'. It will be the first step towards some constructive proposals for the reframing of the ecclesiological debate in feminist theological terms. These are: the preaching of the word, sacramental celebration and participation in God's being in the world, and God's story with humanity and the whole of creation. Closely connected with the latter is a reclaiming of the communion of saints and with it a renewed emphasis on writing women's church history. As a social institution which has not only been a space of oppression and marginalization for women, but created and indeed continues to create meaning for women, the church has been a space where women have created and continue to create spaces for their own discourses of faith and spirituality. These are, amongst others, discourses of justice, mysticism, prophecy and poetics. Feminist ecclesiology can be understood as a fundamentally subversive activity which seeks to point out that ecclesiological discourse needs to be much more complex than traditional and main/malestream theologians have anticipated. Poetics, justice, mystic spirituality and prophetic ministry need to be put on the agenda of the church's reconsideration of its own identity. As liberation theologians have pointed out, ecclesiology cannot take place disconnected from ecclesial praxis, from what happens in the church and where women find their place and their identities within it. This needs to be illustrated again by looking at another set of boundaries: the boundaries between church, world and the kingdom of God. Feminist ecclesiology has provided an analysis of the over-concentration of mainstream ecclesiology on the church as an institution. The church as an institution is often experienced by women as a space of fundamental injustice. Within the church we need a framework for analysing injustice and creating justice for women as well as for telling the stories of injustice and oppression. But we need to go further than that: Letty Russell proposes 'justice' as a fifth mark of the church. Such a concern for justice needs to transcend the boundaries of the church as an institution and seek to transform it into an open space where justice is found, but also into an institution which by its very nature takes a counter-cultural stand in advocating justice for the whole of creation, both human and non-human. I propose a critical, creative and constructive reading and rereading of ecclesiology which is both radically feminist and radically catholic. Though perhaps not invited to the mainstream of ecclesiological debates, it does, however, seek to be radical in reminding the church of aspects of its teaching, its tradition and its spirituality, which it has a disturbing tendency to forget.

The final chapter makes a different form of a constructive proposal. Going back to the notion that feminist ecclesiology is both a subversive activity within existing ecclesial and ecclesiological frameworks and a constructive activity, I want to propose a feminist narrative ecclesiology. Ecclesiology is not about the creation of an institution or a 'club', but about participation in a narrative, the telling and retelling of the story of creation and redemption, the story of the Triune God told in the multiple and diverse stories of women. Such a narrative ecclesiology does not seek to play off the concept of a 'church of the word' against a sacramental ecclesiology, but it makes the vital connection between the two through the lives of women, through women's bodies embodying the body of Christ.

Feminist ecclesiology is an embodied ecclesiology that celebrates the diversity of women's bodies being the body of Christ. This book presents feminist ecclesiology as a discourse that responds creatively to existing theological and institutional contexts and that widens and expands these to a celebration of diversity and difference.

# Chapter Two

# The Ambivalent Legacy of History

Church history, as it is conventionally taught in universities, theological colleges and seminaries, is not women's history. At best, some notable women, exceptions of course, are mentioned, but most of the time women are confined to being the silent majority, objects which are not worth a specific mention, rather than subjects of history. For example, we hear about Henry VIII's dissolution of the monasteries, but tend to forget that the dissolution of convents, was in fact the end of one of the few opportunities for recognized status available to women in the church in England. Martin Luther and other Reformers married former nuns whom they had 'liberated' from their convents and redefined the role of the godly woman as one who gave her life in childbirth and service to her husband and master. Yet we hear little about the experiences of these women and whether they saw themselves fulfilled in their new roles.

Writing history is a process of selection and selective interpretation in order to make sense of the present. The process of selection is guided by the question: what matters for our interpretation of both present and past? We need to ask: what matters in our writing of church history? If we affirm that women are church and have always been church, this means that women matter, that women's bodies, their lives and stories, their discourses of faith are the matter of what it means to be church and therefore are what matters in our reading of the history of the church. If the church—the historical bodies of both mainstream churches and other bodies in which meaningful discourses of faith have taken place for women—is the community of women and men, we need to find ways of writing the history of the church which take account of this more complex and diverse understanding of church.

In this chapter, I will provide a brief overview of the history of Christianity in its institutionalized form, reflecting how women have been affected by the various transformations in the self-understanding of church and how they have both participated and subverted the institutional church in order to make space for their own discourses of being church. The purpose of this chapter is to develop an understanding of feminist readings of church history which can be the basis for a feminist understanding of the church.

The writing of feminist ecclesiology is the work of both a theologian and a historian. Different institutional churches recourse to particular periods in the history of the church, such as Early Christianity or the Reformation, as a means of justifying their current praxis and identity. Often such a recourse to history also becomes a means of justifying the exclusion or subordination of women in the lives of particular denominations. Feminist ecclesiology therefore needs to engage with such selective interpretations of history in order to challenge them and, where necessary, to show their patriarchal distortion and bias.

One question asked by feminist scholars writing on women's Christian history is whether the conventional ordering of church history into periods such as the Early Church, the Middle Ages, the Reformations and the Modern Period actually makes sense for women and authentically reflects their experience of being church or whether it attempts to confine, select and order women's discourses of Christian faith into yet another man-made framework. Elizabeth A. Clark, a historian of women in early Christianity, cites Joan Scott as arguing that '"women can't just be added on without a fundamental recasting of the terms, standards and assumptions of what has passed for objective, neutral and universal history", for that view of history "included in its very definition itself the exclusion of women"' (Clark 1999: 90).

## Reconstructing Christian Origins?

The reconstruction of Christian origins, of the beginnings of early Christianity, as a time in history in which women participated equally in the life and ministry of the church, a reality later to be destroyed by patriarchy, has been on the agenda of feminist theologians for some time. Its most prominent representative is Elisabeth Schüssler Fiorenza who sees the equality and prominence of women in the Jesus movement and in the Early Church as the basis of the *ekklesia* of women, an understanding of church in which women participate fully in all decision-making processes. Fiorenza's first major contribution to the development of feminist critical theology and hermeneutics was her classic *In Memory of Her: A Feminist Theological Reconstruction of Christian Origins* (Fiorenza 1993a). In this book, first published in 1983, Fiorenza challenges previous conceptions of Early Christianity as distorted by the patriarchal agenda behind conventional historiography. She describes the earliest Christian communities as followers of the vision of Jesus, which was one of social justice and equality. Even though this vision has been distorted by the increasing influence of patriarchy in the church, it has never entirely vanished and can therefore be re-visioned for the restoration of the contemporary church.

The theme of the reconstruction of the church of the New Testament has, however, not only been used by feminist theologians, but even more so by Protestant groups of dissenting or non-conformist traditions. Two examples here are the Brethren church, which separated from the Church of England in the nineteenth century over an increasing awareness of decline in the latter, and the house-church movement in contemporary Britain, which sees its task in the eschatological reconstruction of the reality of the churches of the New Testament and essentially the restoration of the kingdom of God. 'Restorationism' means doing the historically impossible, to re-enact the pure reality of the Early Churches. Their understanding of the Early Church in fact provides a political agenda for what is to be enacted in the present and to justify it by claiming historical authenticity for it. Fiorenza's approach fundamentally differs from that of the restorationist or the Brethren movement.

While both Brethren and house-churches assume an objective reality of an early Christian non-institutional church which proclaimed the authentic gospel and can be found by a literal reading of the Acts of the Apostles as well as the Pauline and deutero-pauline epistles, Fiorenza and others engage in *feminist reconstruction* of Christian origins. In other words: Fiorenza is conscious of feminism as her political agenda in reconstructing Christian origins. While Brethren and house-churches model themselves on the hierarchical structures described in the household codes of the New Testament as their archetype, feminist authors like Fiorenza value the *equality* exhibited in what she reconstructs as Christian origins. And here it is important to note both that she reconstructs something called the 'Jesus-movement' and that she does not remain limited within the boundaries of the canonical Scriptures of the Christian Testament. The groups taken as examples here build their understanding of 'reconstruction' on trust in their interpreting the canonical sources as describing historical reality 'as it was', which equals 'as it ought to be'. Fiorenza fundamentally mistrusts andro-centric historiography, which denies the presence of women as active participants in early Christian communities (Fiorenza 1993a: 70). She describes her understanding of historical reconstruction connected with 'social interaction and religious transformation of the Christian "vision" and historical realisation, of struggle for equality and against patriarchal domination' (Fiorenza 1993a: 92). The prototype of a vision of equality and justice for all needs to be built and modelled in each particular historical situation and can therefore never be embodied by one particular historical institution alone.

The recourse to Early Christianity as it is practised by groups like the Brethren or the house-church movement could also be understood as the search for 'authenticity', the search for a way of being church which resembles that of the earliest followers of Jesus more closely than that of the mainstream church. From a feminist perspective such a search for authenticity as a model, be it historical reality or a social construct, is essentially doomed to failure as it does not take into account the reality or the particularity of the lives of those who are church now. They, and this applies to women in particular, as they have not been included in the process of (re)construction, which is often rather to their detriment than to their gain, become degraded to mere actors with a walk-on part rather than those who embody Christ through their particular embodied sexual being. Fiorenza is aware of this danger and tries to achieve greater flexibility and awareness of the context by her concept of the life and vision of the Early Church as prototype, a vision which is continuously being embodied in many different ways throughout the history of the Christian Church. For her, the life of the Early Church is a political agenda rather than a selective reconstruction of reality which makes that reality appear in a light that is to the advantage of those in power. Becoming aware of the reality of the continuing vision of alternative ways of being church and women's constructive presence in them is a first important step towards a feminist reconstruction of ecclesiology that takes account of, and reclaims, the Christian tradition and the ecclesiological debate within it.

Fiorenza refuses to accept the marginalization of women in history as a complete description of historical reality, but understands it as reflecting androcentric historiography and choice of sources rather than what actually happened (Fiorenza 1993a: xvi). Therefore all sources available and made canonical are to be treated with equal suspicion as being influenced by a particular, patriarchal agenda. Patriarchy for Fiorenza is not restricted to male domination over women, but she describes it as a network of oppressive structures which along with sexism/heterosexism include racism, classism and ageism:

> *Patriarchy* as a male pyramid of graded sub-ordinations and exploitations specify women's oppression in terms of class, race, country, or religion of the men to whom we 'belong'. This definition of patriarchy enables us to use it as a basic heuristic concept for feminist analysis, one that allows us to conceptualize not only sexism but also racism, property-class relationships, and all other forms of exploitation or dehumanization as basic structures of women's oppression (Fiorenza 1984: xvi).

She understands patriarchy as any kind of hierarchical structure which seeks to define women only in their relationship to men. In her later work, Fiorenza prefers the term 'kyriarchy', which describes a more refined concept of domination and of those who are victims of it. Kyriarchy is a network of domination and rule of some human beings, be they men or privileged women over others. This means that the commitment of women-church cannot simply be defined as 'women' over against male domination, but we have to speak of a much wider commitment to all victims of oppression and domination. This implies Fiorenza's use of the spelling wo/men in order to express the fragmentation and particularity of women's lives shaped by structures of class, race, sexual orientation and religion as factors constructing women's social identity (Fiorenza 1995: 24).

Fiorenza's refusal to accept the marginalization of women in the church as a given fact does not mean that she does not acknowledge the oppression of women throughout the history of both church and society, but she refuses to accept it as an entirely representative picture of reality, as it neglects the fact that women have always been present in the church and have always sought to resist patriarchal structures (Fiorenza 1985: 134) as well as to create spaces for their own discourses of faith within the church. She argues that the egalitarian vision found in the earliest Christian movements has never been completely extinguished despite the competing influences of patriarchal tendencies:

> The remembrance of women's sufferings in religious patriarchy must be explored structurally in order to set free the emancipatory power of the Christian community which is theologically rooted neither in spiritual sexual dimorphism nor in patriarchal ecclesial dominance, but in an egalitarian vision and in altruistic social relationships that may not be 'genderized' (Fiorenza 1993a: 92).

She draws a picture of early Christianity which views it as being in constant tension between the vision of radical equality and women's full participation in leadership, in other words as being an alternative to existing Graeco-Roman society, and the increasing influence of the cultural values of the surrounding society, 'the gradual adaptation to the patriarchal order of the Greco-Roman society' which 'robbed the church of its clear-cut social boundaries vis-à-vis its prevalent patriarchal cultural-religious norms and environment' (Fiorenza 1993a: 303). So Fiorenza understands the adaptation of patriarchal structures, such as monarchical episcopacy, not so much as a gradual process of distortion of originally pure egalitarian structures, but as a struggle in tension between two competing powers, in which patriarchy eventually gains hegemony, but the original egalitarian vision is never lost entirely and can therefore be reclaimed. Fiorenza understands the gradual acceptance and domination of sexist attitudes and structures as well as the refusal to let women participate in church leadership not only as a sin from which the church needs to repent as it left behind racism and its support of slavery, but a denial of the catholic and apostolic identity of the church (Fiorenza 1993b: 88).

Fiorenza uses a constructive rather than a descriptive approach to early Christianity. This means, she does not seek to identify and reconstruct the Early Church 'as it was' in order to construct a model of the church 'as it ought to be', but rather seeks to identify a particular vision of liberation and equality which then serves the purpose of a critique of the contemporary Christian community as well as a vision to transform both church and society. The purpose of Fiorenza's project of reconstructing Christian origins is not to re-enact the pure and true church, whatever shape it might take, but to construct a political and hermeneutical agenda which has its prime locus in the reclamation and transformation of present ecclesial structures.

The enactment, rather than mere *re*-enactment, of the concept of the *ekklesia*, the discipleship of equals, is the foundation of Fiorenza's feminist ecclesiology. The history of the earliest Christian communities is, like that of any other period of Christian history, one of ambiguity for women. An ideal state of total equality never existed. Fiorenza identifies a vision of equality and she and others have found evidence for women's ministries and writings in the life of the Early Church which are means of empowerment for women today. Yet these must be read together with stories of exclusion and the development of patriarchal structures and theological reasoning for women's exclusion. Groups in which women played an important role and were involved in leadership such as the Montanist or New Prophecy movement in the third century, led by Montanus and two women prophets in Asia Minor, were particularly prone to being branded as heretical. Ironically, it was this particular group which the church father Tertullian joined when he perceived the mainstream church as being in decline. Tertullian had previously identified women as 'the devil's gateway'. And yet Fiorenza and others point out that the spirit of women's presence and the vision of equality were never entirely quenched and women continued to make space for their discourses of faith throughout Christian history.

## The Mediaeval Church

The Middle Ages, a period which spans about a thousand years of history of the Western Church, are often described as the 'dark ages' and in many ways they were indeed dark for women. The papacy was gaining increasing power and Aristotelian philosophy, which clearly branded women as being inferior to men, increasingly dominated theological thinking. Women were excluded from the official ministry of the church and from entering its clerical hierarchy. And yet it is this time in particular which saw the rise of an independent women's spirituality particularly in the context of monastic communities.

Prudence Allen in her description of the 'Aristotelian revolution' in Western theology and philosophy highlights an alternative tradition which existed and was manifest in the life and thought of women such as Hildegard of Bingen (Allen 1985).

Hildegard lived from 1098 to 1179 and was founder and abbess of a community in the Rhineland. She insisted on founding her own monastic house in order to ensure that the women under her leadership would not be dependent upon or dominated by men. She also was an adviser to her local bishop and even to secular leaders such as her patron, the emperor Frederick Barbarossa. Hildegard did not begin to write until she was 43 years old. She undertook four tours during which she preached to audiences of both laypeople and clergy, women and men. Hildegard became a prolific writer not only on matters of Christian doctrine, but also wrote extensively on matters of medicine and biology. She was a defender of orthodox theology and was at one stage even asked to write against the Cathars, a group branded heretical by the institutional church of her time. She also composed liturgical music for the nuns in her care. In fact, she argued that those who imposed silence in the church without having a legitimate reason to do so, would not hear the voices of the angels in heaven praising God when they got there. She was, however, intent on maintaining the independence of her own conscience and her own community against the authority of the institutional church where she felt that this was necessary. Shortly before her death, she agreed to the burial of a nobleman who had been excommunicated in the churchyard of her monastic community. As a result, an interdict was placed on the whole community which meant that until the interdict was lifted, Hildegard and her nuns could not receive the Eucharist and were not allowed to practise their liturgical chant. This essentially meant that they were deprived of everything that was at the heart of their life as a religious community. Hildegard, however, insisted on her position even at the risk of her own excommunication.

It is in the visions of Hildegard herself that we find a woman's contribution to ecclesiological thinking which was largely ignored by the male-dominated church of her time. Yet Hildegard wrote firmly within the framework of the theology and ecclesiology of her own time. She did not object to ecclesial or secular authority as such but merely to its abuse. Some of her contemporaries criticized her for her practice of accepting only women and girls of noble birth like herself into her community. Hildegard saw the church as *Ecclesia*, the pure Mother Church and bride of Christ. She wrote:

> ...the Church is the virginal mother of all Christians, since by the mystery of the Holy Spirit she conceives and bears them, offering them to God so that they are called the children of God. And as the Holy Spirit overshadowed the Blessed Mother, so that she miraculously conceived and painlessly bore the Son of God and yet remained a virgin, so does the Holy Spirit illumine the Church, happy mother of believers, so that without any corruption she conceives and bears children naturally, yet remains a virgin (Hildegard of Bingen 1990: 174).

As this quotation indicates, there are a number of aspects in Hildegard's writings about the church, which are difficult to accept for contemporary feminist ecclesiology, as they do not reflect the experiences of actual women and their lives. One example is Hildegard's contrasting of the church and the synagogue, the church as the woman favoured by God opposed to her rival, the synagogue, representing the carnal Jewish people who rejected God's plan of salvation through Christ. Also, Hildegard's understanding of the church is highly clerical and regards the ordering of the church on earth as a mirror image of the hierarchy of angels in heaven. Women are, however, excluded from this hierarchy. However, while Hildegard sees the clergy as fulfilling their God-given role in the divine ordering of the church, she is highly critical about any abuses of power which transgress this order. Even her explicit use of feminine imagery, most importantly of the church as a woman giving birth to her children, has its difficulties for today's feminist reader because of the exclusively heterosexual connotations and the implied gender hierarchy. We will explore this type of use of feminine imagery further in the next chapter. What we do find in the writings of Hildegard is the voice of a woman insisting on her right and vocation as a woman to participate in speaking about the church in theological terms and thereby making a contribution to the writing of ecclesiology and to being church, as well as a woman who is prepared to resist and subvert the structures imposed on her by a male-dominated church.

Many other similar examples can be found. Catherine of Siena advised the Pope to return to Rome and to end the Great Schism of the Western Church in the fourteenth century. She believed that the Pope as the leader of the universal church ought to reside in Rome which she regarded as one of the conditions for the reunification of the church divide by the Great Schism. The reason for her interest in reconciling the leaders of the church was her interest in re-conquering the Holy Land, which had fallen into the hands of the unbelievers a century previously. After she had persuaded the Pope to return to Rome, he asked her to undertake various missions of reconciliation between the cities of Florence and Siena. In order to go on these missions, the Pope had granted Catherine a number of unusual privileges. She was allowed to have a portable altar on which she was allowed to have Mass said even in regions placed under an interdict and she was accompanied by three confessors who were permitted to hear confessions even without the permission of the local bishop. We do have to concede that Catherine's privileges depended upon the permission of male ecclesial authorities of her time, but we do find in her a woman who took her role as a member of the body of Christ and her authority seriously and was not to be silenced even when speaking opinions unpopular with the male church authorities. Long after her death, in 1970, she, together with Teresa of Avila, was elevated by Pope Paul VI to be a 'doctor of the church', a recognized teacher of the faith.

The religious life, the vocation chosen by women such as Hildegard and Catherine, was indeed the space in which mediaeval women as women could gain status and recognition as women within an otherwise male defined church. In the twelfth century in particular there was a rise in the number of female religious communities. The limitations as well as the potential of these developments have to be recognized. Religious houses largely were founded for noble women who recognized their vocation to be outside the framework of patriarchal and often arranged marriage and therefore chose to retain their virginity and devote their lives to prayer and service to the poor and outcast. Due to the restrictions established by the church which excluded women from the ministerial priesthood, female communities were still dependent on the ser-vices of male priests to say Mass and male confessors to attend to the spiritual needs of the nuns and lay sisters. And yet double communities, such as those of Fontevrault in France and Sempringham in Yorkshire, are found in which the female community clearly dominated the male side of the house. The founder of Fontevrault ruled that the leader of the house should always be an abbess who was required to be a widow rather than a virgin, a woman who had had the experience of having a family and contact with its male members. Sempringham was founded by Henry II as part of his penance for the murder of Thomas Becket. This penance included male subordination under female leadership. Nunneries and convents as well as communities of lay sisters were, though within the limitations given by the historical context of the Mediaeval Church, spaces in which women could develop their own desires for a life committed to the church, to education and service to the poor. As such they have to be recognized as part of the history of women's being church within and often despite the dominance of patriarchy within the church.

Another interesting story about a woman getting access to even the highest office in the Mediaeval Western Church is that of Pope Joan. The legend has it that a young Frankish woman with a strong desire for learning took on a male identity, joined a monastery and eventually got to Rome where s/he was elected pope. Her true identity was revealed when she gave birth to a child and subsequently died whilst in a procession. Legend also has it that her name was struck from the official list of popes because as a woman she was regarded as ritually unclean and could not possibly have gained holy orders, let alone have become pope. The official procession which accompanies a newly elected pope to the Vatican still makes a slight detour in order to avoid the spot where Joan is said to have given birth to her lover's child. The Vatican museums also feature a chair with a hole in the seat which was, so legend has it, used to confirm that any pope designate had the right set of genitalia. The story of Pope Joan is a legend and its content of truth remains unknown, but as with every legend it does contain a certain amount of truth not least about the male desire to protect the Mediaeval Church (and the church at any other time in history for that matter) from women's alleged impurity and to retain the ultimate power of church government.

In this section, I have highlighted the stories of three women who are remembered for their presence in the Mediaeval Church. Their being re-membered is largely due to the fact that they entered/gate-crashed male dominated structures of being church. Yet they stand for the majority of nameless women deprived of their power of naming church and being remembered as part of the church's life. Yet the official history of the Mediaeval Church as it is conventionally taught, is largely that of a church increasingly dominated by the Papacy and Scholasticism in which women are hardly mentioned. Yet enough evidence can be traced, albeit in the stories of those women who are remembered, to rethink and rewrite the story of the Mediaeval Church as one in which women were present and which women being church today can claim as part of their heritage.

All of these women, however, did end up having some form of say in more formal aspects of the church of their time. I therefore want to add a fourth example of a woman who lived her life much more on the margins of the life of the official church and yet has been very important for the rethinking of women's spirituality in the twentieth century when her work was redis-covered. Julian of Norwich was a fourteenth-century anchoress, a woman who might earlier in her life have been married with children, but spent the later part of her life as a solitary, living in a small cell attached to the parish church of St Julian in Norwich. Very little is known about her and her life. In her *Showings* she describes herself as illiterate and unlearned. Against the Lollardic heresy of her time, she affirms her own loyalty to the beliefs of 'holy church', as she calls it. Scholars recognize her possible connection with the Beguines, a group of women who, whilst not formally joining a convent, lived together and engaged in charitable work and prayer, particularly in the cities ridden and partly eradicated by the Black Death. Even though Julian, possibly in anticipation of possible criticism, denied being a teacher, she did, however, believe that God had spoken to her and that she should share her 'Showings of Divine Love' with her audience. In addition, she, like all anchoresses, was available for spiritual and practical advice through one of the small windows of her cell. One of the few external references to Julian's life outside her own work is in the book of Margery Kempe who records her visit to Julian and Julian's advice to live a celibate life with her husband after she had been suffering the spiritual and physical traumas of having given birth to 14 children. Julian's cell had three windows: one to the outside, a parlour window and one to the parish church through which she could follow the saying of Mass and receive the sacrament. The life of the anchoress symbolizes the place where much of women's spirituality has taken place throughout history, on the margins of both church and world and at the same time as a bridge between them. On the one hand, Julian was an obedient disciple of the church of her own time, represented through her confessor. Yet, on the other hand she was a 'wise woman' given to prayer, choosing to opt out of patriarchal marriage and relating to other women, sharing her wisdom and knowledge with them and enabling their own discourses of faith and life.

## The Reformation and Its Followers

The Reformations of the sixteenth century are seen as the founding event of their renewed, truly Evangelical churches, by the churches which call themselves Reformed or Protestant. It has to be asked whether such a reading of Christian history is true for women with regard to their being church. Were the events that are now called the Reformation a liberation for women? Did its claims to return to the roots of the gospel enhance women's being church? And are women represented in the writing of the history of the events described as the Reformation?

The Reformation, sometimes seen as the purging of the Western Church from unscriptural traditions, robbed women of two essential forms of representation within the Christian Church: the religious or monastic life and the identification with Mary, the mother of Jesus. While the Early and Mediaeval Church provided an alternative for women who did not feel called to marriage and motherhood, the Reformers asserted that women could achieve salvation through childbirth. The focus of the new religion was no longer the church as an institution beyond the local congregation but the patriarchal family in which the father was responsible for the spirituality of the members of his family, his wife, children and servants. The new emphasis on the preaching of the word of God did not include women as preachers, even though the Reformers stressed the importance of the education of both boys and girls from a young age in order to be able to read Scripture. So, women were permitted as passive readers of Scripture, though not among those who proclaimed the gospel of salvation publicly.

Unmarried women were regarded with suspicion, as entering the religious life was no longer a possibility. The dissolution of the religious houses deprived women of formal representation within the church and the recognition of their vocation to ministries other than within the framework of the patriarchal nuclear or even extended family. Until the late nineteenth and early twentieth century there were very few to no opportunities for women's ministries, ordained or lay. The first ordinations of women took place in the Unitarian, Baptist and Congregational churches during the latter half of the First World War. As these denominations agree on the independence of the local congregation, a local church could call a woman to the pastorate without necessarily having the approval of a wider national or international body. Within the Church of England, women had no recognized ministry until the re-establishment of the religious life in the nineteenth century and the ordination of women to the diaconate and the priesthood at the end of the twentieth. For more than three centuries, this particular denomination deprived itself of the vital contribution of women and restricted women to being passive recipients rather than agents of their being church. Even when these communities of women did emerge, there was ample evidence of male bishops regarding them as a threat to the church and its alleged right to order women's lives of faith (Mumm 1998).

Péri Rasolondraibe comments on the absence of women in the Reformation as it is recognized and claimed as the heritage of churches that exist today:

> When we talk about the Reformation, we always talk about 'his-story' and we learn very little about what women did during and for the Reformation. In the few things written about the women of the Reformation, we can learn, for instance, about Catherine von Bora Luther, who on some decisive occasions and in spite of

the prevailing prejudice against women helped Martin Luther move towards the
right decisions. I have no doubt that there would have been a great difference in
the way the churches of the Reformation were organized, nurtured and structured
if women like her had had more room to act (Rasolondraibe 1997: viii).

Some women, such as Luther's wife, Katharina von Bora, a former nun who
left the convent which she had entered as a child to marry the reformer and
run their extensive household, are recognized in their own right though only
as helpers to the cause of the Reformation, mainly confined to the household
and the giving of hospitality and shelter as well as childbirth. Katharina Zell,
however, is an exception. From an early age, she herself took an interest in
learning and was encouraged by her parents, friends and fellow citizens of her
native Strassburg. Her early biography shows parallels with that of Luther
himself as she devoted her whole life to the search for peace with God
through good works, only to find that peace eventually in hearing the message
of the Reformers. She married the Reformer Matthew Zell and, being
childless, was able to continue studying and corresponding with the scholars
of her time. Most of Zell's life, before and after the death of her husband,
however, was not devoted to scholarship but to practical care of those around
her, be it hospitality or visiting the sick and prisoners, as well as, for example,
complaining to the Magistrate about conditions in a syphilis hospital which
she visited to take care of one of her nephews. Similar to Hildegard of Bingen,
Zell did not allow herself to be confined by the boundaries set by the male-
dominated church. She preached to the women of Strassburg in the cathedral
and even insisted, with the support of other women, on the canons toning
down their loud singing while she was preaching. She protected those who
chose not to follow the orthodox Lutheran way. In 1562, shortly before her
own death, one of her friends, a follower of the radical Reformer Schwenck-
feld died. As Zell found out that the local Lutheran pastor refused to conduct
the funeral, she herself, though already ill and weak, conducted the service
outside the city walls. She was only saved by her own death from the harsh
reactions of the members of the Magistrate who could not tolerate this simple
and pragmatic act of resistance and solidarity of one woman for another and
felt threatened in their own authority by this woman's insistence on her
own ministry.

Women did, however, dissent and sought to recreate the spaces for their
own being church of which the male Reformation had deprived them. Chrisman writes about communities of nuns in Strassburg who refused to leave
their convents and the religious life to which they had committed themselves
(Chrisman 1972). In 1638, Anne Hutchinson was excommunicated from her

congregation in Boston for holding regular weekly meetings in her home to discuss the Sunday sermon and to express her theological opinions. These small gatherings, churches within the church, emerged in a number of different traditions following the Reformation. Many of them were led by women.

One tradition in which women's leadership and ministry had been established more or less from the beginning was that of the Quakers. Quakers believed that the divine light, the spark of God's presence, had been given to all, women and men alike. Therefore they preached radical equality between the sexes from the very beginnings of the movement in the late seventeenth century. Women like Margaret Fell offered hospitality to visiting preachers and were imprisoned, like their male fellow believers, for their support of dissenting religion. Margaret Fell became the nurturing mother of the nascent Quaker movement and helped found its women's meeting. It was often in dissenting and non-conformist movements, outside the established church that women found space and a voice to proclaim their faith. It is no coincidence that Quakerism, which proclaimed the radical equality between men and women, emphasized a strong practical and social justice component of the Christian faith. Women and men share rights as well as responsibilities within the Quaker community. Elizabeth Bathurst, one of the early Quaker women, wrote:

> As male and female are made one in Jesus Christ, so women receive an office in the Truth as well as men, and they have a stewardship and must give an account of their stewardship as well as the men... (Society of Friends 1995: 43).

It is this commitment to radical equality which still attracts women today to explore Quakerism and Quaker meetings as a space where they can find room and a voice which they are denied in their own faith communities.

As these case studies of women's being church through the history of Christianity have shown, women have, within or on the margins of the malestream church, claimed their own spaces. In the fourth chapter of this book, I will discuss how women in the last few decades have taken up this tradition and gone a step further towards forming their own Women-Church. Yet, before I do this, another group of reflections on the tradition is needed, that of a critical rereading of those official theological discourses of being church which male theologians have sought to impose on women. It is to these that I now turn.

# Chapter Three

# Models and Metaphors of Ambiguity and Alienation: Traditional Ecclesiologies under Feminist Scrutiny

Ecclesiology is the theological reflection on what it means to be the church. Such reflections have been undertaken by theologians throughout the history of the church in order to create a normative theological understanding of the church both as it is and as it ought to be. Women have largely been excluded from this process of definition, but this exclusion does not make the definition process and the images and metaphors used any less relevant for women. Images and metaphors used in ecclesiological discourses claim to describe something in which women participate, something which women are and always have been: the church. Most theologians in their attempts to speak about the church in theological terms draw on a number of core metaphors and theological concepts. In this chapter I will evaluate these metaphors and the realities they invoke when read from a feminist critical perspective. I want to ask whether the theological language and ideas traditionally used by male theologians speak about the church in a way which is meaningful for women and describes the church as a liberating and life-giving reality for women and enhances the celebration of women's being church. This involves the search for counter-patriarchal and subversive readings of traditional ecclesiologies in order to reclaim the existing churches as spaces for women's discourses of faith. All theological language is metaphorical language describing a reality that is larger than what can be confined to words. Metaphors are forms of speech, images that are used to describe something in a way that is suggestive of another, in other words: in order to consider the way we speak about the church we have to take into account the realities and images that are evoked and created by the metaphors we use.

This chapter works on the assumption of the contingency and changeability of the core metaphors of ecclesiology, of their being influenced by particular cultural contexts in order to create a patriarchal socio-symbolic order. It is this patriarchal socio-symbolic order which feminist theologians seek to challenge and to replace by a concept of church in which women can live as the particular sexual human beings that they are. In this chapter, traditional ecclesiological concepts are being brought into creative dialogue with the ideas of feminist theologians as part of a creative and constructive rereading of the Christian tradition, which I understand to be at the heart of feminist theology.

The methodology employed in this rethinking of traditional ecclesiological concepts is based on the work of feminist hermeneutics, the critical reading of the Christian and Hebrew Scriptures, as well as on feminist political theory. Before I begin my evaluation of particular concepts, the basic premises of my methodology need to be outlined in brief.

The church as a subject of theological discourse can be seen as a mirror in two ways: on the one hand it mirrors the respective theologian's concept of other aspects of his (*sic*) theology, such as Christology or Pneumatology, and at the same time it reflects the situation and the need of reform of a church at a particular time. The purpose of this chapter is on the one hand to analyse the significance of the church's self-reflections in the wider context of theology, and to evaluate their potential as sources of women's alternative ways of thinking about their being church. Feminist theology is concerned with providing two vital aspects of theology for women and of women: to reflect on the theological significance of women's discourses of faith in order to incorporate them into what is perceived as the body of Christian tradition and to develop theological discourses that are relevant and life-enhancing for women. Building on these premises, the study of ecclesiology combines the two aspects in order to develop discourses of being church that reflect women's being church. A critical reading of ecclesiology therefore takes place given the ambiguity of ecclesiology being a male-dominated discourse and the church being a vital space of life for women. This ambiguity can also be understood, parallel to feminist critical readings of Scripture, as that of the church being at the same time a space of oppression and a site of liberation. If the church is supposed to be a space of liberation for women, then we have to ask whether we can identify the traditional theological language used to describe the church as describing the church as a reality of liberation for women. At the same time I want to develop strategies of liberation and change in order to liberate the texts themselves from being texts that describe an institution which oppresses and marginalizes women and excludes them from all essential processes of representation and self-definition.

Such a feminist reading is always a biased reading, but it seeks to overcome the myth of 'objectivity' which is claimed by conventional ecclesiologies as theologies of the church which speak for all of its members in all their diversity. It takes its starting point from what we have identified as the fundamental premise of all feminist ecclesiologies: that women are church and have always been church. It is not Scripture or a particular understanding of Scripture and the Christian tradition which is the measure of our reading of ecclesiological texts, but our reading is one that seeks to advocate women's presence and representation in theological reflections on the church.

Another reason for engaging in ecclesiological discourse is that the church as the community of women and men also becomes an important transfer point of power between men and women. A feminist analysis is therefore necessary in order to identify the gender-power interaction between human beings in an institution as important as the church. I identify sexuality as a hitherto neglected dimension of ecclesiology and argue that because of this neglect, dominating and oppressive power structures could develop.

Feminist critical analysis takes place in a space of fundamental ambiguity between identification with the church and the necessity of developing alternative structures, claiming that women are church and demand for themselves the right to define what church is. Traditional ecclesiological concepts are still relevant for women, as they are expressions of a church with which women at least partly identify, even though women have, despite the texts claiming to speak for women, not been participating in this process of self-reflection. Such a feminist critical reading is therefore always a *subversive* reading and essentially often a reading 'against the grain' of the given text. Its purpose is not to define the nature of the church in terms of its timeless essence or even to identify the theology of the church of a particular author, but to overcome the notion of 'legitimate' ways of doing ecclesiology by reclaiming the significance of women—as authors, as readers and writers/ poets with authority—being church (Althaus-Reid 1993), and to create and develop an ecclesiological *écriture féminine*.

What I am seeking to develop initially is a feminist critique of traditional ecclesiological discourses. While the previous chapter outlined the ambivalence of presence and exclusion, which goes through the whole of two thousand years of history of the Christian Church, by showing both examples of women's creating their own spaces within a male-defined church and even attempting to participate in the process of defining it, this chapter will analyse those processes themselves. Feminist thinking always begins with analysing women's presence and practices before moving on to the underlying theories and concepts which define and essentially confine these practices.

Seyla Benhabib understands the tasks of a feminist critique as both an 'explanatory-diagnostic analysis of women's oppression' and an 'anticipatory-utopian critique' of the norms and values of our current society and culture (Benhabib 1987). For the purpose of the present study, a feminist theological critique of traditional and contemporary ecclesiologies, I suggest three steps based on Benhabib's understanding of critical social theory: such a study has first of all to provide an 'explanatory-diagnostic' *analysis*. This analysis identifies that up to the present, theological studies of the church have ignored the relevance of questions of gender identity for a theological study of the church, but at the same time they have worked with strong explicit as well as implicit constructions of gender that are culturally contingent, but sanctioned by their use in an ecclesiological context. From there a feminist theological critique has to move on to the *deconstruction* of the results of the first step. The third step will then be a *reconstruction*, or in Benhabib's words an 'anticipatory-utopian critique'. In other words, out of the ambiguity that arises for women from some aspects of the texts studied, we can attempt to *construct* different and feminist *constructive* ways of reading the text that open possibilities of multiple forms of ecclesiology. Two thousand years of history of women's presence and participation in the Christian Church as such suggest that these discourses are too important, or even too meaningful for some women to ignore.

So, what are these metaphors of alienation? What images are used by traditional theology in speaking about the church and what impact do they have on the lives of women as church?

## The Church as Feminine

The origins of this image, which describes the relationship of Christ and the church as that of a man and his humble subservient and pure bride, go back to the Christian Scriptures. The author of the *Letter to the Ephesians* challenges his male readers to love their wives 'as Christ loved the church', in other words: in terms of self-sacrificing love that is even prepared to die for the other. This is, however, preceded by a corresponding challenge to married women to 'obey their husbands in the Lord'. Throughout the history of Christian theology it has been this latter image which has predominated the experiences of most married women; the female is ordered to be humble and submissive to the male. This is ultimately modelled in the relationship between Christ and the church, which authors such as Louis Bouyer and Hans Urs von Balthasar describe as the 'fundamental structure of the universe' that is ultimately 'beyond metaphor' (Bouyer 1985). In other words, the heteropatriarchal ordering of relationships between women and men is beyond question and it is to prevail the whole of society and therefore also the church as the model of an ideal society. This pattern has been used to justify a static ordering of gender and sexuality which understands heterosexual marriage as the only justified form of relationship between two people. Even those who by ecclesiastical law or choice are compelled to abstain from any committed relationship to another human being are defined in terms of the absence of heterosexual partnership or the substitution of a human partner through a disembodied spiritual one, be it the church for the celibate priest or Christ for women religious.

Bernhard of Clairvaux (1090–1153 CE), reformer of monasticism and theologian, proposed to read the book of the Song of Songs, originally a collection of secular love songs ascribed to King Solomon, as a description of the intimate love of Christ and the church. This reflects the process of disembodiment which takes place in the use of metaphors such as the church as the bride of Christ. According to Bernard and others following him, it is not the goodness of mutual love or even sexuality that is expressed through them, but rather a hierarchical relationship between men/priests/pastors who represent masculinity and thereby Christ and women who are to conform to a pattern of feminine submissiveness and false humility.

This is coupled with the idea of ritual purity. Even though the church is portrayed as feminine, even at times as a woman, it is one of her most fundamental characteristics that she is not like other women. The church as feminine and bride of Christ does not have a woman's body. This is reflected in the fact that the male-dominated church can suffer being described in terms of femininity, but has throughout its history shown ample inability to cope with the reality of women's bodies. The bride of Christ does not menstruate and is not defiled by the blood shed in childbirth. The bride of Christ is also represented through the mother of Jesus, Mary, the Virgin and Mother, which I will discuss later in this chapter.

The image of the church as woman and bride of Christ has been used as in recent Roman Catholic moral theology in defence against feminist theology, which is regarded by some as a distortion of Christianity. This is closely connected with concerted efforts to silence the debate about the ordination of women in the Roman Catholic Church by constructing a theological and ecclesiological framework that renders such a debate impossible. The bride of Christ metaphor becomes part of a rhetoric of the supposed dignity of women as long as they perform their childbearing function or fit into the pattern of virginity and denial of their female sexuality.

One example of the potential for abuse of this feminine imagery of the church is the work of Monica Migliorino Miller. Miller describes salvation as actualized by the nuptial union of Christ and his bride, the church, as its proper symbol (Miller 1995). The nuptial union of Christ and his church becomes the essential order of creation and redemption, which are possible only through the submission of the feminine, the inferior, to the male, the head of the church and the whole of creation. Miller distinguishes between male and female authority within the church. Female authority is exercised where women take their place within the church through performing their essentially feminine roles as wives, mothers and virgins. If women fulfil these particular roles, they exemplify the very being of the church, the virginity and motherhood of the church, personified in Mary the mother of Jesus and, in an extended form, in every woman. According to Miller, male and female sexuality are symbols of the nuptial covenant between Christ and his church enacted in the sacrifice of the Eucharist. The active part of that nuptial covenant, however, has to be played by a celibate male priest (in other words a priest who keeps away from sexual contact with actual women's bodies). Male sexuality, which in Miller's estimate is essentially 'exterior' and giving, represents the kenotic sacrifice made by Christ, while 'interior' female sexuality represents the passive, feminine, receiving identity of the church. The aim of Miller's argument is to show how a female priesthood is a violation not only of the authority of Christ, but of the eucharistic sacrifice which is at heart of the very being of the church.

In her concept of gendered authority, Miller understands gender as an ontological category inherent in human nature and based on the analogy of the nuptial covenant between Christ and the church. Miller's ontological understanding of gendered human nature therefore depends on a biological essentialism which makes the possession of male or female genitalia the most prominent feature of human existence. Miller does not take into account that being a man or a woman cannot be perceived outside a socio-biological and linguistic framework of interpretation of gender categories. In her analogy of the relationship between Christ and the church she equates biological sex and gender and thereby makes one particular form of culturally contingent human sexuality the foundation of her understanding not only of human but also of ecclesial authority.

Closely connected to Miller's ontological construction of gender is the fact that her theology is based on a fixed system of gender relationships, a system of compulsory heterosexuality, itself unexamined and treated as beyond criticism, even if we were to agree with her as to its normative character. In a concept in which a nuptial relationship is the fundamental structure of the universe, all other forms of human sexuality are rendered either deviant or essentially non-existent. If the church, according to Miller, cannot be church without the exercise of female authority, even if it only takes place within the narrowly defined structures of patriarchal ecclesiology, how can the church be the church without the voices of those who find themselves outside such an essentially heterosexual discourse?

Miller essentially blurs the categories of biological sex and gender by using the two indiscriminately. Even though she uses the categories of 'male' and 'female' authority, such terminology is actually a contradiction in terms, as authority as a matter of fact cannot be derived from biological sex, but at best from a particular way of constructing categories of gender. Miller tries to subvert this by using categories of biological sex as the foundation of her understanding of authority in the church as the basis for ontological truth claims. These in effect support a particular patriarchal power system rather than the lives of women and men as church.

The most central and important criticism to be made about Miller's theology is that of her attitude towards actual women. Interestingly enough both John Paul II and Miller refer to the lives of 'real women'. But what they do refer to are not women's lives, but rather women as long as they perform particular roles, roles which are defined within a strict and exclusively heterosexual and culturally contingent pattern of gender relationships. Women, as Miller describes them, embody the motherhood of the church, but Miller's description of ecclesial motherhood does not bear much resemblance to the reality of being a mother in different cultures. 'Motherhood' remains an abstract and therefore a disembodied concept. Furthermore, even though Miller refers to the femininity of the church as embodied in the lives of women—in effect of women when they are mothers, brides or virgins—the femininity of the church appears as the exaltation of a *dis*embodied sexuality. The roles chosen for women who embody the church are essentially *asexual* roles, even though they are only described in relation to the absence or presence of a sexual relationship with a man. As such the concept of the feminine church appears to be fundamentally alienating for women who are church as they have either to deny their sexuality before they can be part of the 'embodied' church, or attend to their relationship with other males, not with other *females*.

The exaltation of disembodied female sexuality, in effect its denial, creates boundaries between women in the church rather than enabling them to celebrate the diversity of women's lives and different ways of being woman as the embodiment of the church. It creates a hierarchy between those women who, according to Miller, embody the church and those who might attend the church, but may never live up to being counted into the patriarchal gender-power structure which is established in systems like this one.

Parallel to the denial of women's sexuality is the way in which male masculine sexuality relates to the authority of the priesthood, which, according to Miller, is essentially 'masculine authority'. The theological concept of the 'nuptial mystery' and the femininity of the church support and exalt one particular form of disembodied masculinity. One could in fact speak of the exaltation of 'sexuality without sex', for the masculine priestly authority is exercised through a celibate male who is essentially 'married' to the church, the disembodied bride. Luce Irigaray, one of the few feminist philosophers actually interested in Christianity, describes the shortfalls of this image very perceptively:

> Being a mother is but one possible mode of woman's service to Jesus; he lacks a wife. Defining her as the Church, as Israel is defined as the bride of Yahweh, is tantamount to saying that Christ is wed to his work alone, which is not the fulfilment of humanity but a model of the patriarchal and the phallocratic (Irigaray 1997: 200).

The concepts of ecclesial maternity and priestly paternity seem to substitute fathering or mothering with the exaltation of parenthood without pregnancy, childbirth and without children.

## Mary, Personification of the Church

Mary, the mother of Jesus, has been one of the most ambiguous aspects of Christian (and particularly Roman Catholic) theology and ecclesiology for women. While Mary on the one hand represents the 'feminine side of the divine', she also represents an ideal which real women are unable to reach. On the one hand, Mary acts as 'intercessor', as the one who is closer to her son, who will not reject her requests on the behalf of human beings; on the other hand, she is also virgin and mother at the same time: female but without sexuality. Therefore Mary becomes the personification of disembodied femininity, the woman who is what no woman can ever be: virgin and mother at once. As such Marian symbolism can be and is abused as an instrument of male power over women, as a means of disciplining women through an unattainable ideal. Such a form of Marian theology allows Mary to be church, but not women.

Mary has often been seen as the supreme personification of the church, the ideal disciple, in the church and yet its mother. Otto Semmelroth, following the tradition of church fathers such as Ambrose and Augustine, sees Mary as the 'type of the church' (Semmelroth 1963). Both Mary and the church are seen as the 'new Eve'. Standing under the cross, Mary becomes not only the mother of Christ, but also gives birth to his body, the church. The mediaeval theologian Hermann of Tournai describes Mary as the neck of the body of Christ, the mediatrix between Christ the head and his body the church and yet a full member of the body (Graef 1963).

Rosemary Radford Ruether summarizes the use of Marian symbolism in traditional ecclesiology:

> Mariology…is the exaltation of the principle of submission and receptivity, purified of any relation to sexual femaleness. Virginity expresses the male quest for spiritual rebirth, freed from carnal femaleness that represents the tie to mortality and finitude. The church is a virgin mother in whose womb we are reborn to eternal life, freed from the mortality of human maternity. Thus official Mariology validates the twin obsessions of male fantasies toward women, the urge to both reduce the female to the perfect vehicle of male demands, the instrument of male ascent to the heavens, and, at the same time, to repudiate the female as the source of all that pulls him down to bodiliness, sin and death. Mariology exalts the virginal, obedient, spiritual feminine, and fears all real women in the flesh (Ruether 1979: 4).

Some male theologians see the personification of the church in Mary as a counterbalance to a concept of church which is dominated by an emphasis on structures, hierarchy and institution. Leo Scheffczyk, for example, points out that the

> 'Marian principle', the principle of serving devotion and humble receptivity, provides a genuine balance and enlargement of the hierarchical principle that tends to be one-sided. The inclusion of Mary as Virgin and Mother in the order of salvation imparts on the church, which is the outstanding place of continuing salvation, in a totally special way, profoundly sensitive, deeper human maternal and even mystical characteristics. Arrayed with such characteristics, the Church can provide to men of all states and dispositions the protection, the security and the familiarity which flow from a maternal virginal being (Sheffczyk 1988: 100).

Aims such as these are also pursued by feminist theologians working on the transformation of the theological understanding of the church. Yet we have to ask whether an understanding of Marian symbolism which essentially serves to deny women's sexuality and to support the existing male-dominated hierarchical structures can really be a means of transforming structures which would allow women full participation in the life of the church.

The status of Mary as the supreme personification of the church and its most honoured member is used as an argument against women's admission to the ministerial priesthood. Mary herself, though the highest of all human beings and the supreme personification of the church, never participated in the hierarchy or demanded to be ordained priest. So if Mary was not granted admission to the priesthood, why should women? Monica Migliorino Miller argues that 'the Marian principle' is one of the foundations of a truly sacramental and masculine priesthood (Miller 1995). Such an understanding of the significance of Mary in the church transforms a female symbol into a means of women's alienation from being church. Mary being understood as the type of the church and indeed its most prominent member can on the one hand be understood as a theological way of honouring women and affirming the significance of women in the church, but on the other hand Mary being totally church, means that she is not Christ and therefore cannot be regarded as representing the female within the divine. As a woman she cannot be divine although her supreme qualities are described such that she is what no woman can ever attain to be. Kari Børresen comments on this typology:

> What this typology does…is to *transpose the androcentric system from the order of creation into the order of redemption*. It presupposes the socio-cultural patriarchal distinction between male and female roles, and then, within the typological couple, casts the human partner—Mary or the Church—in the instrumentally child-bearing, i.e., specifically female role, and the divine partner, Christ, because of his pre-eminence, in the specifically male role… I would argue that *the theme of the new Eve*, a historically conditioned human formulation, *is now an anachronism*, and that to go on using this anachronism is pernicious, because it helps to perpetuate ecclesial androcentrism (Børresen 1983: 50).

Therefore Mary as the personification of the church can only serve for women to take their place, where patriarchal ecclesiology wants them to be within a church, with which they cannot identify on their own grounds.

On the other hand the significant role which Marian spirituality has in fact played for women compels me to see Mary as an important symbol which has been claimed and reclaimed by women as the presence of the female at a vital position in Christian theological symbolism. Mary is, after all, a woman who reminds us of, and affirms the necessarily inevitable presence of, women in the church. As a number of feminist theological discussions on Mary have shown, it is possible to apply a method of deconstruction and rereading to Marian symbolism in order not to discard what is, after all, a vital symbol for women (Halkes 1983; Johnson 1985; Maeckelberghe 1989). The importance of Mary as a person and a symbol for both ecclesiology and women shows that it is not possible to think of a sexual ecclesiology without reclaiming Mary for women in the church. Feminist ecclesiology has to recover the history of women's subversive Mariologies for itself.

Rosemary Radford Ruether suggests replacing existing power structures which reflect structures of domination within society with those of social justice and a 'preferential option for the poor'. Through this preferential option for the poor, which is symbolized by the Mary of the Magnificat, structures of equality and justice can be implemented in the church. Women who are often the primary victims of poverty and oppression then become models of faith and their liberation becomes an issue of supreme urgency, in fact the primary concern of the church (Ruether 1983). In her earlier work she argues for a reinterpretation of the relationship between Mariology and ecclesiology. Rather than understanding the Marian symbol/the church as the symbol of the feminine, the inferior, Ruether sees Mary as the symbol of the new and liberated humanity which has essentially overcome patriarchal dualistic binary structures (Ruether 1975). Mary's song, the Magnificat, proclaims Mary and all women as the ones who experience the end of their suffering and disempowerment, their liberation through the message of the gospel. This message, however, is not only for women, but proclaims justice and liberation for the whole of humanity. This is the message which the church embodies and proclaims through its very existence.

Together with the image of Mary as the supreme personification of the church, comes the idea of Mary, and therefore the church, as the new Eve, the one who atones for and replaces the sin of the first Eve which resulted in the expulsion of humanity from the Garden of Eden and close fellowship with God. Eve, the first woman, though created from Adam's rib, was a sexual human being, defined through her relationship with Adam and ultimately through her sexuality being his peril. While Christ, according to the apostle Paul, is the new Adam, the church becomes the new Eve. This symbolism suggests the denial of all female-defined human relationships with symbolic, asexual relationships. Even the mother of humanity ultimately led humanity into peril and was punished for it through her pains in childbirth, associated with connotations of the impurity of all female blood shed in menstruation and childbirth. Relationships with natural mothers therefore need to be replaced by pure, new relationships with the church as the pure, new mother which denies the presence of female sexuality in the bringing about of all human life.

Yet the use of Mary, after all a real childbearing woman, as the supreme personification of the church, is also a reminder of the exclusion of women and their suffering from traditional ecclesiological reflections. Gavin D'Costa refers to Margaret Argyle's picture of the Bosnia Christa that depicts a crucified woman on the background of a vagina. Argyle created her image as part of her response to the mass rape of Bosnian women at the hand of Serbian soldiers. D'Costa reminds us:

> The unspoken, unshaped ecclesiology implicit in Argyle's representation, and it must be unrepresented, is that not until such women as the Bosnian rape victims have experienced healing can the church dare to call itself the risen and glorified body of Christ. The women's bodies, as well as the male rapists' bodies belong in different ways to the body of Christ—and without their redemption, without addressing their sufferings, which form the 'lack' in Christ's afflictions, all flesh is not yet redeemed (D'Costa 2000: 64).

While most theological reflection on Mary, the mother of Jesus, has traditionally been situated within Roman Catholic theological discourse, it is also significant for our feminist theological reflection on the Church that the Protestant Reformation almost entirely obliterated Marian devotion and spirituality from its own understanding of Christian theology. As a feminist theologian, I have to ask whether this could be regarded as a symbol for another attempt to counteract and deny all female presence, be it actual or symbolic, from what shapes the Christian Church. Even though the twentieth century has seen a certain amount of Protestant interest in Mary, partly due to developments in the area of ecumenical dialogue, much of this interest has been focused on aspects such as the virgin birth. The latter is, as Rosemary Radford Ruether points out, primarily a doctrine about Jesus, in other words, it perpetuates the denial of Mary as an actual female human being and therefore as a symbol which could be meaningful for women in their reconstruction of the Church as a community in which women's lives and sexualities are embodied and celebrated (Ruether 1979).

Any personification of the church, be it as Mary or as the new Eve, remains ultimately problematic as it exalts one person to be the supreme ideal of anything any member of the church is meant to be and yet, due to their sexual identity and nature cannot achieve. Personification perpetuates oppressive hierarchical gender patterns and deters attention from the reality and diversity of the lives of those who are church. Being church expresses a form of corporate identity which entails diversity among its members. It not only exalts the absence and denial of female sexuality, but also points to the supposed superiority of maternity and motherhood which is the experience of some women but by no means of all. Motherhood is in itself an ambiguous experience, as is the experience of being mothered. Feminist theologians have pointed out the problematic nature of the use of paternal language and imagery for the divine, but have also largely abstained from simply replacing 'father' with 'mother' in an unqualified way. While the experience of parenthood as well as being a child is, of course, an important aspect of being human, women's identity cannot be reduced to it. Luther argued that women could obtain salvation through bearing children. Today's religious right propagate so-called 'family values' as part of an agenda which identifies the place of women as being between 'children, cooking and church'.

The concept of the personification of the church in Mary as its supreme disembodied realization is detrimental to an understanding of church as community which affirms a diversity of human relationships as healthy. Feminists argue that we need to emphasize the values which make those relationships healthy, in other words mutual affirmation and justice, not one particular relationship as the fundamental relationship on which other relationships are essentially modelled. Mary as the model of the church undermines the full humanity of women and men in their diversity and particularity in the image of the divine which in itself is essentially being in relation. A Marian ecclesiology in the traditional form exalts women's being regarded as only of secondary value and subservience over against male dominance and power.

## The Church as the Body of Christ

In the previous section on the gendered conception of the church as the feminine bride of Christ and mother of all believers, I have referred to the essentially disembodied nature of such metaphors. This also applies to another very prevalent metaphor used with regard to the church. In 1 Cor. 12, Paul describes the church as the one body of Christ, which has many members that perform different functions, but are all part of the same body.

Even though the church is described as feminine, when it comes to using body imagery, it has to be a *male* body which becomes the place of salvation. This is an expression of the alienation which women often experience in the church: they are required to deny their sexuality, their bodies, their humanity, their womanhood in order to be regarded as part of the church. Salvation is regarded as only possible through the body of a man. The Christian Church throughout its history has seen a significant number of female ascetics who aimed at ridding themselves of their femaleness, their embodied being, in order to become male and thereby to obtain salvation. Caroline Walker Bynum writes about mediaeval religious women who starved themselves to the point of their menstruation stopping altogether in order to rid themselves of their female impurity (Bynum 1987). In a saying added to the apocryphal

Gospel of Thomas, the author has Jesus respond to Simon Peter, who had challenged Jesus to make Mary Magdalene leave the disciples: 'Look, I will guide her to make her male, so that she too may become a living spirit resembling you males. For every female who makes herself male will enter the kingdom of Heaven' (*Gos. Thom.* 114). This saying, similar to the body of Christ image, shows that women are part of the church, the group of disciples following Jesus, though not as they are, but only if they come to reject their bodies and their identities as women in order to assume a male body. This is alienation in the fullest sense of the word.

The Anglo-Catholic theologian Claude Chavasse writes: 'She [i.e. the church] is only the body of Christ because she is also the Mystical Bride of Christ' (Chavasse 1942: 71). Such a mixing of metaphors reflects the confusion and utter repulsion with regard to women's bodies which some aspects of traditional ecclesiology express. It shows the utter dependence of the feminine church on its male head, Christ, a disembodied man. This is not merely an example of oppressiveness of gender relationships within a hetero-patriarchal social symbolic order; beyond that it shows how the types of gendered imagery used as and when necessary perpetuate that order. The church can be the bride of Christ, defined through her relationship with him, but as soon as body symbolism is employed, the picture has to change, and only a male body can represent the pure church. Such negative 'body theology' can and has become a means of alienating women from their own bodies. In addition, through replacing the reality of women's lives and women's bodies, being church is substituted with a corporate disembodied feminine which ultimately serves to alienate women from each other.

The metaphor of the church as the 'body of Christ' suggests that women are required to deny their own bodies and become part of a new, different and male body in order to obtain salvation. Such metaphorical language and imagery cannot be separated from the experience of women in the church, manifested, for example, in the liturgy. What does it mean for women that on the one hand they have, through baptism, the symbolic new birth, and have become part of the body of Christ, but on the other are denied access to its assemblies after their own bodies have been rendered temporarily unclean by giving birth themselves? The rite of 'churching', both a rite of purification and of thanksgiving after childbirth, which can, for example, be found in the *Book of Common Prayer*, is regarded as a readmission of women to the worshipping community after a period of supposed impurity. Orthodox churches still deny menstruating women access to the Eucharist. Married Orthodox priests are also to abstain from sexual relations with their wives prior to celebrating the

Eucharist. In order to retrieve the idea of the church as the body of Christ we have to define the church in a way which affirms and celebrates women's bodies as part of this corporate body and which understands the church as incomplete without them. Embodiment is most strongly expressed through the sacramental tradition within Christian theology which has traditionally been part of ecclesiology. This will be discussed in Chapter 6 which shows its importance as the key to reconsidering and reframing the ecclesiological debate in a feminist framework.

## The Church as Servant

Dietrich Bonhoeffer points out that the church can only be the church if it exists for others. Shortly before his death in 1945, he wrote:

> The Church is the Church only when it exists for others. To make a start, it should give away all its property to those in need. The clergy must live solely on the free-will offerings of their congregations, or possibly engage in some secular calling. The Church must share in the secular problems of ordinary human life, not dominating, but helping and serving (Bonhoeffer 1967).

In doing so, he stands in a long tradition of those who point out that the church cannot exist unless it takes its relationship with those outside it seriously and follows Christ's example of existing 'not to be served but to serve'.

While, on the one hand, Bonhoeffer's argument continues to pose an important challenge to the church in an age of secularization, this quotation cannot be read by feminist theologians without challenge as it does not reflect the experience of women working for the church.

Feminist theologians would certainly agree that the church has to engage in matters of human life as, from a feminist perspective, there cannot be a distinction between 'secular' and 'spiritual' matters. The messages given about the human and particularly the female body in traditional Christianity seem to suggest such a distinction, as women's bodies are rendered unclean and in need of purification and sanctification. Feminist theologians, and a church which takes the challenge posed by them seriously, have to question those messages given by the whole of society about the place of women and the way women's lives are shaped by concepts of femininity and male dominance.

This metaphor of service as a description of what makes the life of the church is again fundamentally ambiguous for women if read in the context of women's experience both in society and in the church in particular. Women have often found themselves called to subservience and service and have seen their lives regarded as of no value other than to exist for the sake of others, be it their husbands, their children or even the church. The kind of surrender of, for example, financial privileges is in fact what women have to a large extent experienced and been asked to do in giving their lives to the service of the church. In the context of the Church of England, for example, a female ordinand is much more likely to be asked to engage in unpaid or non-stipendiary ministry, if no appropriate stipendiary post can be found, than a male ordinand. On the whole, women, both lay and ordained, are the ones who are giving large amounts of time and unpaid service to the church. Here, we have to ask whether such an understanding of 'unpaid service' is really helpful and just: unpaid work is largely seen as second rate and suggests that women are in fact in a position to do so as it presumes that women have other sources of income available to them, such as a husband's salary. This does not reflect the reality of women's lives in the contemporary world. A further question to be asked is whether or not this actually ties in with the church's calling to challenge structures of injustice in society if the church exempts itself from legislations ensuring equal opportunity for members of both sexes and countering discrimination on the grounds of sex. While on the one hand Bonhoeffer's challenge to the church to surrender unnecessary and extensive wealth in order to support justice and equal distribution of resources is an important message to be heard and followed, the church also needs to be challenged with regard to its own distribution of resources within its structures.

Theologians using the servant metaphor in their understanding of the church identify the life of the church with that of Christ: Christ was the one who gave his own life for the salvation of the world and so should those who are church. I have to ask here, whether the life of Christ as it is presented in conventional theology, is really a useful role model for women. The experience of women seeking help in cases of abuse and violence at the hands of their husbands, often reflects their being told to identify with the suffering of Christ rather than to challenge their abusers and to withdraw from situations of abuse. I have to ask whether the self-denying suffering of Christ is the message which women need to hear or whether it condones and perpetuates structures which are indeed sinful and require eradication. In her work on Paul Tillich and Reinhold Niebuhr, Judith Plaskow suggests that the concept of sin in fact has different meanings for women and men (Plaskow 1980). While 'male sin', according to Plaskow, is indeed arrogance and pride, the reality of women's experience suggests rather the opposite: a false humility and self-denial, the eradication of their personality and the denial of the sacredness of their being in the image of the divine as women. Later feminist thinkers have tied this in with a structural rather than an individual understanding of sin. I therefore have to ask whether an understanding of the church as servant does not perpetuate rather than challenge and subvert structures of sin and injustice within both church and world.

In his theology, Bonhoeffer tried to challenge the church out of its complacency and self-centredness, its primary concerns with matters of ecclesial politics and ritual. While this is a necessary message to be heard and one which is endorsed by feminist theologians, I have to ask what kind of a relationship Bonhoeffer and others following him, suggest between the church and the world. The servant metaphor works on the assumption of a radical differentiation between the church and the world, which it serves and aims to subsume under itself. For feminist theologians such a distinction is not tenable as it suggests the possibility of withdrawal from matters of justice and social transformation prevalent in 'the world'. Such a distinction supposes a hierarchical distinction between church and world rather than a constructive dialogue between different groups and institutions. The church can only assume a prophetic and essentially subversive role which enables it to challenge structures of injustice in the world and to transform them if it is itself willing and able to listen and to identify those structures of injustice in its own quarters. I therefore have to ask what concept of the relationship between the church and those outside it is at the heart of the servant concept. Is it one of mutual relation or one of hierarchical opposition?

As women's experience seems to suggest rather the latter, I have to ask whether what is suggested here is a one-sided christological orientation of thinking about the church which is inevitably hierarchical and therefore unhelpful as it perpetuates the kind of gendered binary structure which feminism seeks to subvert. Along with general developments in ecclesiological thinking going on elsewhere, feminist theologians need to explore the possibilities of a more Trinitarian ecclesiology which explores concepts of mutual affirmation of personhood in relation with mutual giving and receiving. I will explore this possibility further in the last chapter of this book.

Furthermore, I also have to take account of the question of where women's discourses of faith and spirituality take place, and I find that the experience of contemporary Western societies such as the UK and the US suggests that the primary location for such discourses is to a large extent no longer within the institutional church. A feminist reconsideration of ecclesiology has to take account of both institutional and para-institutional discourses of women's faith and spirituality. This means that a distinction between church and world as it is suggested by the servant metaphor is essentially unhelpful and alienating as it no longer reflects women's experiences of Christianity in their complexity.

While Bonhoeffer and other theologians influenced by him propose a church 'for others', feminist ecclesiology envisions a model of church where those involved can be church 'with others'. The church is not an inward-looking community which leaves the poor in their poverty and extends only charitable giving to them, but a community in which all are welcome as the people they are and all gifts are valued as contributions to the reign of God. It is a community in which justice is practised. Justice, however, does not merely mean the equal distribution of goods by those in power, but rather a community in which all are welcome, in which every body is celebrated as part of the body of Christ, a gathering of those who are church together with others. In a feminist community, difference is among the key values. A feminist community is not based on 'helping' others, but on being with each other in the image of the Triune God.

### The Church as Gathered Worshipping Community

While traditional ecclesiologies have to a large extent tried to think about the church in terms of its relationship with Christ, its head, Lord and master, thereby introducing and maintaining the kind of hierarchical and potentially if not explicitly gendered binary structures, more recent ecclesiological thinking has focused more extensively on those people who are church and thereby define its nature. The feminist concept of Women-Church, which I will discuss in more detail in the next chapter, takes its basic idea that women are church and have always been church, from liberation theology's concept of base ecclesial communities. The Second Vatican Council defines the church as the 'people of God', a metaphor not unproblematic in itself. Feminist theologians tend to think of the church as a community made up of particular individuals who hold a more or less firm commitment to this community and its aims. Such an understanding of church as community, even base community, is rooted in the North American tradition of pragmatism and voluntarism, and takes little or no account of the church in terms of its institutional structures or the universal nature which is so important for the Roman Catholic tradition, for example. This is in part a response to the institutional abuse which women have experienced from the hands of hierarchical institutions such as the Roman Catholic magisterium. It also reflects the forms of institutional exclusion which women still experience, such as the refusal of the Roman Catholic Church to ordain women to the ministerial priesthood.

A community ecclesiology defines the church not only in terms of the people who are church but also in terms of what these people do; they worship God and orient their lives according to the Christian gospel as proclaimed through preaching and the celebration of sacraments. I must, however, ask whether this understanding of the church as Christian community meets women within and on the margins of the Christian tradition in their experience of being church, or whether their experience of being church is not much wider, as worship must intrinsically be connected with justice and the proclamation of the Christian gospel can only be good news for women if it affirms their full humanity in the image of God.

Traditional ecclesiology has also always held that the church exists as both local and universal church. The universality or catholicity of the church is not only understood in terms of geography but also as transcending categories of space and time, earth and heaven. Women can therefore not allow themselves to restrict their discourses of being church to only the local gathered communities in which they participate, even though their experience of participating in the discourses of faith which take part in these communities do manifest their being church in most concrete ways and such experience must be the starting point for any reflection on being church. Feminist ecclesiology is essentially a process of rethinking and reclaiming existing concepts as well as creative and constructive development of new models and methods. Such a dynamic process in critical and constructive dialogue involves the possibility of reclaiming what is or might be meant by ideas such as universality and catholicity as well as the praxis of diverse gathered communities.

I also have to bear in mind the fact that the concept of community itself can be highly exclusive. The feminist philosopher and social theorist Iris Marion Young points out that a narrow-minded focus on community can itself be alienating for women and others. In her essay 'The Ideal of Community and the Politics of Difference', Young criticizes the model of community as a concept of radical politics and proposes the 'city' as an alternative model (Young 1990b). Building on Young's work on the 'politics of difference', I want to discuss whether the emphasis on small base communities does not inevitably entail a certain ecclesial and theological provincialism which disguises rather than enables the importance of difference. Young defines her concept of the 'politics of difference' as laying down 'institutional and ideological means for recognizing and affirming differently identifying groups in two basic senses: giving political representation to group interests and celebrating the distinctive cultures and characteristics of different groups' (Young 1990b: 319). For my current purpose of reconsidering the church from a feminist perspective, I want to identify the character of sexual difference, of the dimension and relevance of gender, as a special case. The point is that women cannot simply be understood as yet another group represented in the 'unoppressive city' which Young proposes as an alternative model to the ideal of small communities. Therefore, it is mainly her critical argument about the ideal of community on which I draw here.

Young gives four reasons why a model of community cannot work and in fact is not desirable. First, she suggests that a community model denies the difference between subjects. It assumes equality between the members of the community which does not reflect the reality. Such a model denies what Young calls the 'irreducible particularity of entities which makes it impossible to reduce them to commonness' (Young 1990b: 304). A feminist theological critique points out that human beings are in fact different but that in the context of Christian theology and praxis this difference cannot be the basis for exclusion or marginalization but is rather a factor of enrichment for the church. Feminist ecclesiology has, first of all, to be a celebration of the different bodies participating in the life of the church. In a context where women are reflecting theologically on the experience of being branded 'the Other', feminist re-constructions of the church should take on as one of their central concerns the development of a positive understanding of particularity, difference and multiplicity. Theologically such an affirmation of difference and particularity must be grounded in an understanding of Christ which describes Christ not only as the guarantee of the unity of the church, but also prevents such unity from being gained only at the price of diversity.

The second aspect of Young's criticism is that any community identifies itself by excluding or not reflecting on those who are not part of the com-munity. She points to these dangers by comparing the community model with racism, ethnic chauvinism and political sectarianism. Community-based models like Women-Church or the base communities in Latin America often focus so much on those who are in the community and their participation in the life of the church, that little attention is given to those who are not part of the community. This became particularly obvious in the history of the Women-Church movement, which on the one hand claimed to represent the first time in history women claimed to be church, but at the same time received a number of complaints from black women, Hispanic women, native American and women-identified women (i.e. lesbian) who felt unrecognized and unrepresented in their particular experiences of being women. Being aware of the danger of a certain kind of ethnocentricity which is inevitable as the dark side of contextual awareness, I want to redefine or broaden the con-cerns that I want a feminist enquiry into ecclesiology to address. Building on my earlier claim that a feminist ecclesiology has to add the dimension of gender to the ecclesiological debate, we have to search for a model which allows for both gender particularity and the ubiquity of gender as a dimension to be addressed. Young does not say that community-based models inevitably lead to issues like racism and ethnical chauvinism, but she maintains that 'a desire for community often channels energy away from the political goals of the group and also produces a clique atmosphere which keeps groups small and turns potential members away' (Young 1990b: 312). A feminist model of ecclesiology has to address the issue of difference in a way that allows for gender differences to be celebrated in the church as a whole and in its different parts, without viewing the small cell or community as the only centre where being church can and does happen.

Young's third criticism attacks the equation of mediation with alienation. She points to the fact that a model of decentralized, unmediated small units is both unrealistic and politically undesirable. According to Young, there is no reason to assume that face-to-face relations in a small community are more authentic and unmediated than relations that are mediated in space and time. 'For both face-to-face and non-face-to-face relations are mediated relations, and in both there is as much the possibility of separation and violence as there is communication and consensus' (Young 1990b: 315).

Such a model avoids, as her fourth criticism points out, the question of the relation among such decentralized groups. She argues:

> The ideal of community, finally, totalizes and deptemporalizes its conception of social life by setting up an opposition between authentic and inauthentic social relations. It also detemporalizes its understanding of social change by positing the desired society as the complete negation of existing society. It thus provides no understanding of the move from here to there that would be rooted in an understanding of the contradictions and possibilities of existing society (Young 1990b: 302).

Young sees the danger of the detemporalizing and dematerializing of concepts of interaction and institutions which is also applicable to our reconsideration of ecclesiology from a feminist perspective. If we are aware of the contingency of particular concepts of gender, yet seek to affirm the importance of sexual difference and gender for a possible reconsideration of ecclesiology, we have to take into account the possibility—and in fact the necessity—of change in our thinking about the church. Such change is only possible if we consider the church in its wider historical and spatial context and reflect on the significance of gender from that perspective.

Young does not then deny the value of small communities for human interaction, but rather argues against small communities as an ideal model of organizing society, or in the case of this study, the church. Arguing against the tendency for feminist ecclesiology so far to favour models of small communities, in order to criticize the universal claims of a supposedly universal and impartial church, requires further explanation. While models of small communities on the one hand make greater participation and articulation possible, they on the other hand neglect the dimension of an awareness of the body of Christ as a whole, and of women in their particular situations and interactions with each other embodying Christ. A feminist ecclesiology must therefore seek to embody a 'politics of difference'. The theological justification of such difference, different bodies embodying the body of Christ, is founded in the reality of Christ's incarnation into sexual particularity. One of the reasons to create models of ecclesiology which focus on base community structures rather than on a centralized concept of the church, was to avoid the dominance of one group, in this case that of white male power, over all others. This goal remains. Yet we have to attempt to identify this aim not only in a negative, but also in a positive way. A feminist ecclesiology of difference must not primarily define itself as opposing power structures of oppression and dominance, but must become able to move on to structures which are capable of representing difference, and sexual difference in particular:

> If we give up the ideal of impartiality, there remains no moral justification for undemocratic processes of decisionmaking concerning collective action. Instead of a fictional contract, we require real participatory structures in which actual people, with their geographical, ethnic, gender, and occupational differences, assert their perspectives on social issues within institutions that encourage the representation of their distinct voices (Young 1990a: 116).

The Christian Church as it exists in the world at large and in society in particular is such a political entity. We can therefore not retreat into an ideal of community without speaking of the lives of the actual human beings who embody this community. We need to hear their distinctive voices and hear their stories as the stories of God told and embodied as church. The church as a local gathered worshipping community has, however, been in some parts of the Christian tradition a starting point for resistance and alternative practice as it was able to make decisions about issues such as the ordination of women in the context of that autonomous community without having to seek the approval of a wider national or international institutional body. It is these traditions, together with a wider concept of the church which we need to reclaim.

Serene Jones describes her vision of church as a space in which 'bounded openness is possible'. While she, like other feminist theologians, acknowledges the ambivalence which the church as a site of suffering, marginalization and oppression holds for women, she refuses to give up on the potential that the Christian tradition also holds. She proposes to understand the church as a 'community of radical openness', open to both God and the world. She argues that the very being of the church rests in a play of difference and diversity (Jones 2001). The strength of the church, and therefore the reason for retaining and transforming it as a site of feminist discourses of faith, lies in being able to combine a resilient framework of practices, traditions and beliefs and a radical openness to the voices of those who engage with them as part of their story of life and faith.

Elisabeth Schüssler Fiorenza suggests reclaiming the Greek word *ekklesia*, which describes the assembly of full citizens with the right to vote and participate in decision-making. She prefers it to the word *church*, which is after all derived from the Greek *kyriake*, meaning 'house of the Lord'. Fiorenza points out that '[t]he translation process which transformed *ekklesia*/democratic assembly into *kyriake*/church indicates a historical development that has privileged the kyriarchal/hierarchical form of church over that of a democratic congress or discipleship of equals'. Fiorenza highlights the contradiction which is inherent in the term 'church' as such: it combines the concept of the patriarchal hierarchical structure of the household with the concept of the democratic assembly of free citizens which emphasizes structures of equality and friendship (Fiorenza 1997: 63).

This list of metaphors of ambiguity and alienation is by no means exhaustive but remains inevitably selective. What I have attempted to show is that ecclesiology is a form of theological discourse which is highly gendered and works with imagery that is alienating to women if not reread and reframed in a feminist critical way. In the final chapters of this study of feminist reconsiderations of ecclesiological reflection, I will propose that feminist theologians need to reclaim and refocus the whole of ecclesiological discourse in order to make a contribution to the self-reflection of the contemporary church. But before such constructive proposals for the future of ecclesiological reflection can be made, it is necessary to focus in more detail on feminist reflection and praxis of being church so far. It is to the life and work of some of these movements and communities that I now turn.

# Chapter Four

# Women-Church:
## Reclaiming Women's Being Church in Feminist
## Communities of Worship and Justice

One of the key characteristics of feminist ecclesiology is to refuse to identify any one particular location of women's being church to the exclusion of any other. Women are church whether they choose to remain within existing institutional frameworks or to find other spaces for their discourses of liberation from the restrictions of the patriarchal church. For a large number of women, the patriarchal and institutional church is no longer a meaningful framework. They begin to create new forms of being church often in small informal gatherings of women (and sometimes men) who celebrate liturgies, read Scripture and work for social justice. The women participating in these groups take their spiritual lives into their own hands, refusing to seek permission from the institutional churches they have left behind.

A conference which took place in November 1983 in Chicago, entitled 'From Generation to Generation: Woman-Church Speaks', understood itself to be the first occasion in history in which women publicly and collectively claimed that they are church and sought publicly recognized participation and dialogue with the official church as well as attention to their concerns and issues.

So, what is Women-Church? What are the ideas behind it and how does it manifest itself both outside and on the margins of the existing Christian Churches? This chapter will try to answer these questions by looking at both the history of the Women-Church Movement in North America and similar movements in other parts of the world, as well as the theological reflections of some of the feminist theologians who have been involved in this movement.

In the late 1970s and early 1980s, a number of organizations involved in the struggle for the ordination of women in the Roman Catholic Church had managed to establish a platform for dialogue with the American Roman

Catholic bishops. When, however, this dialogue appeared to show no evident results or move towards changes in ecclesial politics, the Center for Concern, a social justice organization based in Washington DC, called for a national conference of Roman Catholic women working for social justice and transformation of the church. A national conference of the Women's Ordination Conference, originally planned for the same year, 1992, had been cancelled and replaced by a number of more local meetings. The conference organized by the Center for Concern was called 'Women Moving Church' and can be seen as the place where the concept of 'Women-Church' or the *ekklesia* of women was conceived. It marks the shift from women seeing themselves *within the church* to understanding themselves *as church*:

> In planning WOMEN MOVING CHURCH we sought to design a feminist process: a conscious structuring of the conference design to embody the values feminists identify as alternatives to patriarchal structures. These values include community, mutuality, empowerment, wholeness, equality, participation and transformation. These values have the potential to negate the false myths which affect human interaction, namely privatism, hierarchical decision-making, domination, submission, dualism, passivity and co-optation (Riley and Neu 1982: 1).

This transformation of self-understanding can be seen as the first expression of what subsequently became known as the Women-Church movement. In her paper 'Gather Together in My Name… Toward a Christian Feminist Spirituality', Elisabeth Schüssler Fiorenza assesses the impact of the women's movement for Christian spirituality. She formulates the vision of the '*ekklesia* of women' which, according to Fiorenza, was to find its historical embodiment in the lives of Roman Catholic women today. She therefore argues for the transformation of its structures (Fiorenza 1982).

*Ekklesia* is a dynamic term which describes a community where radical democracy is practised. Radical democracy, according to Fiorenza, in fact represents the vision of the earliest Christian communities which, though later submerged by dominant patriarchal ecclesial structures, has never entirely been lost. It must, however, not be confused with existing democratic political structures, or what Fiorenza calls the 'kyriarchal actualization' of democracy, which in fact often have not been concerned with the lives and needs of women and can therefore not be seen as realizations of the *ekklesia* (Fiorenza 1995: 16). Only a feminist model of radical democracy enables Women-Church to become a space for alternative, counter-hegemonic discourses of faith and political commitment (Fiorenza 1995: 28). For Fiorenza, the '*ekklesia* of women' is an alternative vision of what it means to be church, a theological or better hermeneutical concept as well as a political agenda.

The term 'Women-Church' or '*ekklesia* of women' is an oxymoron that 'indicates that *ekklesia* will become historical reality only when women are fully incorporated into it' (Fiorenza 1993b: 196). Women-Church is therefore not an exclusive term with regard to men, but it seeks to make conscious the reality of women's exclusion from ecclesial processes of decision-making. Fiorenza understands Women-Church as the movement of self-identified women and men who identify with women's struggles. Using a term like Women-Church means that the traditional, patriarchal church can no longer claim to be the sole representation of church, let alone to be a realization of the dynamic reality of the *ekklesia*.

Women-Church does not understand itself as a schismatic movement. Its members are reluctant to found new institutions, but try to keep administration and structures to a minimum. It exists as a loose network of a number of groups which claim their Roman Catholic heritage as the background against which their quest for transformation develops. Avoiding the foundation of new institutional structures not only means the refusal to separate entirely from the Roman Catholic Church, but is an expression of the constant potential for change which should be inherent in all forms of Christian community. It represents a certain reluctance to establish power structures which may potentially be abused. It also enables the practice of more participatory models of organization. Because of this conscious decision to do without new institutional structures, no one group can claim to represent the Women-Church movement more than any other, even though, due to diversity with regard to the size of groups involved, power struggles between large and often financially powerful and smaller local groups occur quite frequently. This hesitancy about founding new and alternative structures is also connected with a reframing of the issues on which the movement concentrates. The focus is not so much on providing a platform for official dialogue with the established church, but a space in which women's voices can be heard and women can be empowered to be church in whichever situation they find themselves. It affirms women's identity as part of the church, which cannot claim to speak or act on their behalf nor claim to be the sole and complete representation of the *ekklesia*.

Another reason why Women-Church avoids establishing more than a minimum of necessary structures is the diversity of relationships to the church as an institution being represented within the movement. While a Roman Catholic background initially served as a common denominator of the movement as a whole, some women involved in the movement maintain a strong and close relationship to the existing institutional churches and are actively involved in the life of their local parish, while others have left the institutional church behind and are looking for new and alternative ways of living out their spirituality. The loose network structure which the Women-Church movement claims for itself has also resulted in its development from being a movement of women who claim their Roman Catholic background, to a network of feminists with a variety of different and often ambiguous connections with Christianity. A Women-Church conference held in Albuquerque, New Mexico in 1993, for example, featured over 30 varieties of Sunday morning worship, including Goddess worship, an Indian pipe ceremony, Sufi dancing, a Holocaust remembrance, a Quaker meeting and a variety of feminist liturgies, although there was no Catholic mass (Dorrien 1995: 275). This loosening of its ties with the Roman Catholic Church points to the fact that the concept of 'Women-Church' cannot be seen as the last word on feminist ecclesiology, but that a new reconsideration of the church's understanding of itself in the light of women's presence in the church is necessary.

Apart from the short period between 1978 and 1981, there has hardly been any official dialogue between the institutional church and representatives of the Women-Church movement, though there have been various attempts to address the Vatican which have been ignored by the church authorities. That women are denied ordination to the ministerial priesthood is one example of patriarchy as an oppressive system, but it is seen as a symptom which needs to be addressed as part of a much wider agenda of social justice for women. In many ways, the relationship between the Women-Church movement and the official church has become one of mutual disinterest. There is, however, a strong emphasis on not leaving the church behind entirely, despite the fact that individual members may have chosen to do so or have become alienated from the church. This would mean leaving all power to the existing church structures as well as abandoning a wealth of tradition, especially that of women throughout history seeking to make their own space within the existing tradition (Hunt 1989).

The Women-Church movement seeks to stay in a relationship with the institutional church which is characterized by a certain ambiguity. While total schism and the establishment of new institutional structures is refused, so is a clear answer to the question of whether the women of Women-Church are inside or outside the church. Women-Church is rather in critical dialogue not only with its Roman Catholic background tradition, but also with other traditions, and it is developing a variety of spiritualities of choice and critical evaluation of its rituals and symbols (Ruether 1993a). Rosemary Radford Ruether describes it as one of the central features of the Women-Church movement to be on both sides at once, in critical dialogue with the tradition and at the same time seeking new ways of spirituality (Ruether 1996a). In contrast, Mary Hunt sees the requirement of an either/or, of deciding to opt for or against the church and its tradition and not being given the option of a partial choice or even of participation and structural transformation, as a characteristic of a patriarchal church which no longer has meaning for women (Hunt 1989). Women-Church, for Fiorenza, is a manifestation of the universal church, not a separation from it. As such she understands it as transcending all artificial boundaries between human beings, and between women in particular. These include boundaries of race, class or religious denominations, as well as, for example, the difference between religious and laywomen within the church. Justice is implemented where these divisions between human beings and between women in particular are overcome. Fiorenza draws particular attention to the relationship between 'nun-women' and laywomen. She understands this division as imposed by the patriarchal church in order to create a hierarchy similar to that between clergy and laity. She urges religious women to give up the privileges granted to them by the patriarchal church in order to unite with laywomen in a coalition of 'sisterhood' as the foundation of a renewed and transforming church. Women religious have been in many ways, and continue to be, among the driving forces of Women-Church. I can therefore say that it is one of the main characteristics of the Women-Church movement to create a third option to the choice between conformity and schism, to live in conscious ambiguity with regard to their relationship to the structures, rituals and symbols of the established church. This means that the church is acknowledged as an institution of salvation which cannot easily be left behind or replaced, but which needs to be reclaimed and transformed in order to be a space in which discourses of worship and justice which are meaningful for women can take place.

After the paradigm shift that initiated the theology and history of the Women-Church movement, another smaller, though not insignificant, paradigm shift occurred within the movement. While the 1983 conference was entitled 'From Generation to Generation: *Woman*-Church Speaks', the next conference in 1987 had the motto '*Women*-Church: Claiming Our Power'. The original singular, interpreted as some women attempting to establish a voice which speaks for all women, was changed to the plural which represents the diversity of women from different backgrounds involved in Women-Church. Women-Church began as, and has continued to be, a movement that exists within its North American context and reflects some of the characteristics of this context. This is, for example, seen in its struggle for inclusivity and equal representation of women of different ethnic and social backgrounds.

In many ways, this remains a goal inherent in the strong commitment to social and political justice. Yet, the history of the Women-Church movement echoes the early criticisms made by Black Hispanic and Asian women theologians that feminist theology continues to struggle to move beyond being a movement for white middle-class educated women. It is interesting to observe that issues of diversity and difference have been on the agenda of the European Women's Synod from its very beginning and are central to this movement (Moser 1995: 105). Despite a number of difficulties in actually putting it into practice, it has always been one of the objectives of Women-Church to be open to women from different social, racial and cultural backgrounds, as well as women of different sexual orientations. The embodiment of Women-Church means addressing issues of racism, sexism and classism and replacing them with values of diversity and the celebration of difference. It was one of the main objectives of all three conferences, and certainly of the movement as such, to address the different situations with regard to class, religious experience, sexuality and race in which women live and shape their experience of what it means to be a woman both within, and on the brink of, existing church structures.

Using words like 'church' or 'Women-Church' is not meant to be an expression of exclusivism in any form, be it Christian exclusivism by using the term 'church' or a community that is exclusive of men by calling itself 'Women-Church'. By using terminology like 'church' the representatives of the movement seek to express that the male-dominated church of patriarchy no longer has the right to claim to be the exclusive representative of 'church'. Such an argument can be seen as representative of the movement as a whole. There was, for example, a debate over whether or not ritual meals at conferences should be called 'Eucharist'. There has been no unanimous decision over this issue, for while some understand the use of terms like 'Eucharist', 'ordination' or 'church' as a claim indicating Women-Church as being no more and no less church than the institutional Roman Catholic Church, others point to the hurt that has been done to women by what these concepts traditionally have expressed and argue for the introduction of new terminology as well as entirely new theological concepts of being church. Women-Church is an attempt to reclaim being church as a counter-space to the patriarchal agenda to which traditional ecclesial institutions have subscribed. This implies also the struggle to implement a new vision of equality and justice both within and outside these traditional ecclesial bodies.

The life of the Christian community is only one aspect of reality, which needs transformation. The contemporary political agenda of Women-Church is the transformation of the lives of women in biblical religion, in other words Judaism and Christianity, which are at present subjected by kyriarchal structures, but have never entirely lost the vision of liberation and equality which can be reclaimed from the life and praxis of the Jesus movement. The self-affirmation of women in biblical religion as human beings no longer defined by patriarchy and no longer subject to its structures is the primary goal of the feminist movement in which the creation of the '*ekklesia* of women' is located (Fiorenza 1984: xiv).

Women-Church proposes a vision of transformation and seeks to create spaces in which such transformation can take place. Rosemary Radford Ruether highlights the need for a temporary separation for women from male-defined spaces into oases of liberation in which they can gain confidence in their new visions of liberation, transformation and justice. Some women find such spaces in feminist liturgical communities which meet to celebrate new alternative feminist liturgies and provide space for women to tell their stories of suffering and struggle for justice. The idea for such small communities is taken from Latin American liberation theology and its base ecclesial communities. In the UK, a number of women's networks, such as the Catholic Women's Network or the Catholic Women's Ordination Movement have developed. In local groups and national conferences, women find spaces for sharing of experiences and celebration of their faith as well as a platform from which attempted communication with the wider church or other institutions in society is possible.

While Elisabeth Schüssler Fiorenza coined the term Women-Church or *ekklesia* of women and developed it as an alternative hermeneutical concept to the dominant discourses of self-reflection in the patriarchal institutional church, Rosemary Radford Ruether has been concerned with the actual life of Women-Church communities as temporary spaces of women's retreat from the patriarchal church. Ruether sees the life of the church as being in the constant tension of being an institution, which is in danger of self-perpetuation and stagnation, and being a dynamic charismatic community where renewal and dissent are possible and take place. The starting point of Rosemary Radford Ruether's feminist ecclesiology is the praxis of various feminist liturgical communities, which as liberated zones are in dialectic tension with the patriarchal mainstream church. Base ecclesial communities or feminist liturgical communities are a variety of different groups which develop from the particular needs of those who participate in them and therefore can 'take on as many or as few functions of church as they choose'.

> They might range from consciousness-raising groups that primarily share experi-
> ences, to groups who engage in study and analysis as well, to groups that also
> worship together. From a study, teaching, and worshipping group, such a com-
> munity might also choose to share means of livelihood with one another. They
> might further choose to make their shared spiritual and social life together the
> base of political action (Ruether 1983: 205).

Base communities and parallel organizations provide space for women to develop their own spirituality, theology and work for justice without entirely separating from the institutional church, but at the same time are outside the control mechanisms of its power structures (Ruether 1995: 18-19). Feminist base communities for Ruether are parallel structures on the edge of the main-stream of the church that ensure spiritual survival within the patriarchal structures of the church.

For Ruether, the praxis of base ecclesial communities is the way to approach the inseparability of ecclesial life and political commitment. Even though Latin American base ecclesial communities provide the model for feminist ecclesi-ologies like Ruether's, she emphasizes the need for adjusting this particular model to the particular needs of the situation in which a group finds itself (Ruether 1986a: 56). What is important here is that feminist base ecclesial communities provide a valid ecclesiological model for the development of a feminist counterculture that opposes patriarchy and seeks to develop alter-native structures, but at the same time does not want to separate entirely from the established church, and seeks to make creative use of it in order to eventu-ally transform it.

With regard to the relationship between Women-Church and the institu-tional church Ruether develops the liberation theological concept of the 'exodus community'. The exodus is not to be understood as being an exodus from a church that has become a symbol of patriarchal power, but Ruether sees the exodus community as something the whole church is meant to be: a community on its way from patriarchy to the 'eschatological' goal of a libe-rated co-humanity of men and women. To witness to that goal (i.e. liberated humanity), which Ruether understands as the gospel itself, is Ruether's understanding of the particular vocation of women in the existing structures of the church (Ruether 1987: 79). It is not the church as such from which women—and in fact the church itself—need to be liberated, but patriarchy as an oppressive ideology. The emphasis in Ruether's work, however, remains not on the eschatological goal to be realized, but on the present struggle for liberation, in other words on the praxis of feminist liturgical base com-munities. But it is important here that Ruether identifies the exodus of Women-Church not as an adjunct to the exodus from a male church, but as the first time in history that women collectively claim to be church themselves (Ruether 1988: 57). Ruether argues that in the past, male exodus movements have often resulted in greater liberty for *men*, but not necessarily in an improvement in the situation of women, often even in an increase in their oppression (Ruether 1988: 55). The collective nature of women's exodus is of importance as it represents the rejection of boundaries between women, for example between religious and laywomen, which are imposed on them by the patriarchal ideology which Women-Church seeks to oppose and to overcome.

The Women-Church movement continues to exist, though mainly in the form of the Women-Church Convergence, a loose network of a number of different organizations that share a commitment to goals such as social justice and equality for women and are loosely affiliated with a Christian/Roman Catholic context, though not all of them understand themselves primarily as church groups. Representatives of the member groups meet once a year for a small conference at which current issues are discussed; however, the aim is never to develop a new institution but to put the main effort into supporting local feminist base communities. These small conferences to which the different member organizations send delegates were preceded by three national conferences: 'From Generation to Generation: Woman Church Speaks' (1983) in Chicago; 'Women Church Claiming Our Power' (1987) in Cincinnati; and 'Weavers of Change' (1993) in Albuquerque/New Mexico. These national conferences, which were also attended by some international delegates, were organized as meetings of mutual empowerment and encouragement for women of Roman Catholic background. However, they by no means represent the main purpose of the work of Women-Church, but rather one form in which the life of Women-Church can take place. These conferences should therefore be understood as landmarks in the historical development of the movement rather than as the sole expression of the movement.

It has in fact been a concern at all three conferences to implement participatory models of valuing and encouraging the contributions of individual participants rather than to emphasize the impact of keynote speakers. Much room was given to discussions at conference tables as well as to the life stories of women from a variety of backgrounds. This identifies Women-Church as a base ecclesial movement. It expresses that women are church rather than the church being represented by the hierarchy of persons of theological expertise and warranted ecclesial power.

One member group of the Women-Church Convergence is Chicago Women Church. Their aims and objectives are summarized in the following mission statement:

We, as a sacred circle of loving and powerful women, deeply respect the individual differences of each of us. Each woman is free to hold and express her own views and life journey. We delight in the creativity, growth and joy of one another. We know and share tears, and hold one another through our confusions and pain. We honor and encourage the Spirit in one another to expand and ignite. We are dedicated to the continual exploration of the feminine, thus affirming the feminine in one another. We create safe space for women to explore our growing and the possibilities for change. We value and encourage risk-taking and freedom in ritual experiences. We will allow no boundaries to be placed upon us that hinder or limit our individual self-expression. Going forward as a faith community, we have the following needs:

To respect individual differences

To allow for one another's silent moments

To increase our diversity

To share leadership and responsibility as an egalitarian community

To invest in our continuous formation and spiritual growth

To be open to further exploration of who we are and what we want to be identified as, in various social and political terms

We are a community whose roots are intertwined, growing in many directions. We are searching for the Transcendent in ourselves and in the universe. We celebrate the beauty in others and in our daily environment. The Spirit is generous and blesses us as we ask. We are Goddess—we bless one another as we meet—we share the smile of love—and we are filled. So we name ourselves Chicago Women-Church (http://www.chicagowomenchurch.com/).

Closer to home, in the UK, the London-based St Hilda Community was a space where women met to share liturgies and create a women-defined space for worship and work for justice. The community was founded in 1987 by a group of women exasperated by their experience of sexism in the various churches from which they came. The group understood itself as an experiment in being church. Its history was closely connected with the struggle for the ordination of women in the Church of England. Prior to the ordination of women in the Church of England, the community was a space where women, who had been ordained to the priesthood in other member churches of the Anglican Communion, celebrated the Eucharist. These Eucharists were regarded as illegal by the established church after a measure to permit women 'lawfully ordained abroad' to celebrate in Anglican Churches in England had failed to obtain the necessary majority of votes in General Synod. After such Eucharists had initially taken place secretly, a group of women decided to hold them openly to proclaim their faith in these being rightful acts of worship for both women and men:

> We wanted men, as well as women, to be an integral part of the Community, because part of what we wanted to learn (and to teach the Church) was a more equal and generous way of gender-relating than any of the churches (even those which already ordained women) seemed to understand. We wanted a Community that worked by consensus and not by hierarchy, because consensus was what, as feminists, we had spent the previous decade carefully exploring. We wanted to call the new group a Community, not because we would be living together but because we wanted to share—gifts, ideas, leadership, vision, and perhaps sometimes possessions and money. We wanted to embrace anyone who came to it, and our earliest rule was that anyone who came to a liturgy was part of the Community while they were visiting us (Furlong 1991: 7).

The community was named after St Hilda, a seventh-century Northumbrian abbess who presided over the Synod of Whitby, one of the most foundational events in the history of Christianity in the British Isles. Prior to Hilda's birth, her mother was told in a dream that Hilda would be a jewel that would shine throughout the land. Hilda came to be abbess and foundress of two monastic communities of women and men. The women of the St Hilda Community saw themselves as proclaiming women's spiritual gifts as such a jewel which had not yet been fully recognized by church and society.

News of the newly founded St Hilda Community and its services, which were held in a College chapel on Saturday night, spread quickly through the church press and through word of mouth. Suzanne Fageol, an American priest who was at the time studying in Britain, was asked and accepted to be the Community's priest and to preside at the weekly Eucharists. Yet, at times, when she was not available, the Community as a whole would celebrate communion together. The St Hilda Community sought to provide a space to experiment and to celebrate women's spiritual gifts and their creativity. This was a difficult and at times painful journey for those who participated. Growth and change are key characteristics of the feminist vision of church which the St Hilda Community tried to live out:

> As women's experiences change and grow, so do our ideas about ourselves and God. For those people who honour tradition and stability, this can be exasperating. For those who wish to continue the spiritual journey with short rests in a refreshing oasis, this is exciting. The St Hilda Community is both oasis and journey for many Christians... We struggle with our community identity. We witness to the world our prophetic vision. We do all these things and more from a feminist perspective in the hope that those who have ears to hear and eyes to see will understand and join our dream of creating a new kind of church. It is a

church whose central focus is the people, the body of Christ. It is a church where
equality in the sight of God is given to all women and men because they are the
image of the divine in human form. It is a church which nurtures, nourishes and
encourages each person to find and speak about the God in their hearts. It is a
church which understands that interdependence and an ethic of care are the
primary ingredients of a worship community. For only as we respect one another
in worship and in language can we see ourselves as builders of a new creation.
The kingdom/queendom of God is among us—and is us (Fageol 1991: 25).

Elisabeth Schüssler Fiorenza distinguishes essentially two different approaches
to the concept of Women-Church. First, there is that of ecclesial base communities, feminist liturgical base communities, rooted in the methodological
alliance between feminist-theology and liberation theology, which is most
prominently used by the North American authors studied and evaluated in this
chapter. Second, there is that of Women-Church as 'synod' which finds more
implementation in the emerging feminist liberation theology in a European
context.

There are a number of similar coalitions/networks, both within existing
denominations, such as the Catholic Women's Network in Britain, as well as
transgressing and disrupting man-made boundaries of denominations and
institutional churches through the work of the Ecumenical Decade of Churches in Solidarity with Women or the Women's Synod Movement which
situates women's being church and women's spirituality in their particular
contexts in different European countries and different churches and creates a
platform from which women can then speak out to leaders of different
churches, to women's organizations and to political movements in their
respective countries. To bring together women from different European
countries to discuss their living together in a new Europe in which East and
West are struggling to live together, their spiritualities and to celebrate their
being women together in the light of their differences, was the aim of the First
European Women's Synod in Gmunden, Austria in the summer of 1996. The
same aims were pursued in smaller national synods such as the WISE (Wales,
Ireland, Scotland and England) Women's Synod in Liverpool in the summer
of 1999 or the first German Women's Synod in Gelnhausen in 1994. A second
European Women's Synod is planned for 2002 in Barcelona. The choice of the
word 'synod' describes women's claim to processes of collective decision-
making from which they have hitherto largely been excluded. Women are
claiming the concept of synod, which exists in many different churches, for
themselves and reframing it for their own discourses of being church.
Women's synods show that women's discourses of being church subvert and
transgress the boundaries set by male-defined church structures in order to

create frameworks and platforms in which women can flourish and be in constructive dialogue with each other as well as celebrate their being church. One of the key features of women's discourses of being church is a strong commitment to justice with regard to all aspects of life, such as the economical and social situations in which women live, but also the celebration of different sexualities as an expression of the diversity of goodness in creation.

There are a wide variety of different experimental women-churches. In this chapter, I have only introduced a small number of case studies in order to show their main characteristics. Yet women's struggle to define their identity as being church is not confined to small liturgical communities, but also takes place within the arena of mainstream churches. Most of these small groups avoid any formal leadership structures in order to set women free from the hierarchical structures which they found oppressive within the churches they left behind. Yet, one of the issues that has been on the agenda since the beginning is the question of the ordination of women to officially recognized ministries such as priesthood or pastorate. It is to these that I now turn.

# Chapter Five

# Beyond Clericalism:
## Grappling with the Ordained Ministry

The Women-Church movement, which I have described in the previous chapter, took as one of its starting points a conscious departure from the struggle for the ordination of women primarily in the Roman Catholic Church. Aiming for the ordination of women within otherwise untransformed church structures became regarded as being contented with a token position within continuing patriarchal structures. Many women particularly in the Roman Catholic Church reject the concept of an ordained ministry entirely:

> I think that women should not ask for permission, but simply *do*. Whatever it is the Holy Spirit calls you to do, *do it*. I am a priest by my baptism into Jesus and grace of the Holy Spirit. We don't need women in Roman collars and robes, titled, working to be bishop, cardinal, politicizing to be pope. We need women filled with the Holy Spirit to *be* Jesus where they *are* (Winter et al. 1994: 21).

> What women seek is not ordination into an anachronistic structure but empowerment in new forms of liturgy and community (Winter et al. 1994: 74).

Many women in all-female religious communities struggle with the need for a male priest to be brought into the community to say Mass and to hear the sisters' confessions. Can ordination therefore still be a meaningful part of women's being church?

The ordination of women to the ministerial priesthood continues to be on the agenda of Roman Catholic women, despite various attempts by the Magisterium to silence the debate in recent years. In summer 2001, the first international women's ordination conference took place in Dublin. Several hundred participants from all over the world stated that it was time to break the silence and refuse to obey the ban imposed by the Vatican to even discuss the subject of women's ordination. The Vatican reacted with anger and attempted to silence the debate. The conference organizer, Myra Poole, a member of the Sisters of Notre Dame de Namur, was asked through her superior not to attend the conference and told that if she disobeyed she would be expelled from the religious order to which she had belonged for 42 years. Sister Joan Chittister and her superior were summoned to Rome and threatened in a similar way. 135 members of her Benedictine community in Erie, Pennsylvania, signed a letter of support pointing to the Benedictine tradition of individual responsibility. The prioress of the community, Sister Christine Vladimiroff, wrote:

> Sister Joan Chittister, who has lived the monastic life with faith and fidelity for fifty years, must make her own decision based on her sense of Church, her monastic profession and her own personal integrity. I cannot be used by the Vatican to deliver an order of silencing. I do not see her participation in this conference as a 'source of scandal to the faithful' as the Vatican alleges. I think the faithful can be scandalized when honest attempts to discuss questions of import to the church are forbidden (www.wow2001.org/benedict.htm).

Pressure was also put on the World Council of Churches to withdraw Aruna Gnanadason who was to be a keynote speaker.

The 370 conference participants passed a resolution urging the Pope to restore the diaconate to women in accordance with the practice of the Early Church and to lift the ban on discussion of the issue of women's ordination as well as to encourage women to study for the diaconal and priestly ministries to which they feel called. The 'conference calls on each member organisation of WOW (i.e. Women's Ordination Worldwide) to pursue dialogue with local bishops, religious, priests and laity on the subject of women's ordination in the context of retrieving the discipleship of integrity' (www.wow2001.org/resolved.htm).

Events such as the Dublin conference as well as the Vatican's reactions to it show that the issue of women's ordination is alive and well in those denominations whose leadership does not recognize that vocations to the ordained ministry are not restricted by race, sexual orientation or gender. And yet, within Women-Church it is now regarded as one aim for some but by no means for all women.

There are, however, much more fundamental questions to be considered in this context: if feminist ecclesiology inspired by the concept of Women-Church reflects the struggle for equality and the end of all hierarchical structures as representing patriarchy, can a distinction between ordained and lay ministry be maintained at all? Or does ordaining anyone inevitably lead to what Rosemary Radford Ruether describes as one of the gravest sins of the patriarchal church: clericalism?

'Clericalism' is a form of power structure which attributes all power of sacramental celebration, theological knowledge and decision-making to experts—in other words, to members of the clergy on whom this kind of power is imparted by ordination. Women on the grounds of their sex are excluded from taking on this kind of power. But Ruether does not argue for the inclusion of women into these structures of clerical power, but rather for their transformation or, as she calls it, the 'dismantling of clericalism', as a feminist understanding of ministry and clerical ecclesial structures are diametrically opposed to each other. She writes:

> Clericalism is built upon and presupposes patriarchy. The symbols of clerical power duplicate on the level of ecclesiastical hierarchy the symbols of patriarchal domination of men over women, fathers over children. It is impossible to liberate the Church from patriarchy and retain a clerical definition of the ministry (Ruether 1983: 207).

'Clericalism' creates divisions or hierarchical binary structures which can be seen in Ruether's understanding as the strongest characteristic of patriarchal thinking. Ruether sees clericalism as separating the ministry from mutual interaction with the life of the community, a development which essentially transforms the community into hierarchically ordered castes of clergy and laity (Ruether 1988: 75). Elsewhere she writes:

> Clerical sacramental disempowerment of the people means taking the life symbols of the community's relation to God and claiming that the divine power and efficacy of these symbols belongs to the clergy alone, through a special infusion of this power from God that takes place at ordination (Ruether 1993a: 201).

All binary structures, according to Ruether's concept of patriarchal ideology, are essentially modelled on and resemble the male-female binary in which the male is seen as the dominant, the strong and the normative while the female represents that which at best complements the male. These binary structures create boundaries between human beings which deny the building of a community. They not only exist between hierarchy and laity, between men and women, but are also imposed by a patriarchal system on women themselves. The most important example Ruether mentions here is the division between laywomen and nuns who, on the grounds of denying their female sexuality are understood as superior to 'ordinary' women. The hierarchy-laity binary structure, which is established through ordination and manifested in every celebration of the Eucharist, is also found in the two other areas of marginalization which Ruether identifies: church administration and theological education.

Clericalism represents the sanctioning by the church of one particular order of society which models its structures of organization after a particular secular model of society. Experiences like the following reflect the manifold alienation which is the inevitable consequence of clericalism:

> I am reminded of endless conversations with Catholic women friends about the Church's position on contraception, wrestling with information about the safe period and exchanging names of 'sympathetic' confessors; how the problem came to be confession rather than contraception. The Church as community, in the person of my women friends in the parish and beyond, shared my experience and understood.
>
> I decided that I could no longer trust the institutional Church in its attempts to control my sexual life.
>
> The institutional Church did not share my experience, it was inept. It never said: 'Where is Christ in your life as a married woman, a mother and a worker?' It insisted rather on the pronouncements of the popes, male princes in a male and celibate organisation. These reduced my life to biological meanings in the context of a theology which is at best partial...
>
> The Church's teaching on reproduction alone is a potent way of keeping women restricted to the private domain and under the authority of husband and Church. Also in the institutional Church members are patently not equal. There is a clerical hierarchy which rules a lay church. Women are not admitted to the clerical hierarchy and men are admitted only if they give up the possibility of relating intimately to women (Petrie 1991: 202-203).

This form of ordering both church and society is then theologically justified as the order of creation. In other words clericalism can be seen as the ecclesial embodiment of patriarchal ideologies. Ruether argues for the replacement of existing clerical structures with structures that enable ministries of mutual empowerment and which are based on the aim of making use of the talents of individual believers. In such a form of ministry, according to Ruether, the very being of Women-Church as a community of liberation is embodied.

Ruether criticizes clericalism as one aspect of the patriarchal church which is experienced as particularly oppressive, but she also addresses the question of ecclesial institutionality as such. While Fiorenza uses her development of an alternative vision of being church and its anticipatory implementation as a vehicle for constructing an alternative location for women's hermeneutical and theological discourses, Ruether concentrates on particular questions of creating parallel and alternative structures to the institutional church. The rejection of patriarchy and clericalism as its embodiment do not, however, mean the rejection of institutional structures as such. The development of base ecclesial communities does not lead to ecclesial anarchy, but rather to a reconceptualization of power structures. Authority that is being exercised within the church can no longer be understood as endowed upon a (by ontological necessity, male) person on his ordination, but is rather redefined as functional authority that serves the members of the community rather than supports particular hierarchical power structures for their own sake. Ruether acknowledges the necessity of institutional structures as a pragmatic necessity, but denies the right of particular structures, like the institutional Roman Catholic Church, to claim sole representation of being church. According to Ruether, Jesus founded a movement rather than an institution. Institutionalization therefore is reduced to being a historical necessity which means that 'all patterns of church polity are relative and historically developed, patterned after political and social patterns in the culture' (Ruether 1986b: 105). This implies the radical contingency of all ecclesial structures as well as the need for the church to acknowledge its own fallibility. No church, and it is the Roman Catholic Church with which Ruether is dealing in particular, can therefore claim a monopoly to represent salvation or an infallible teaching of truth. To acknowledge the possibility of erring as well as denying the need for such certainties in favour of a multiplicity of perspectival truths, according to Ruether, is a necessary step towards maturity which the church needs to take, but which is also an important growing process for women in their claiming to be church and becoming agents of their own faith (Ruether 1995: 14-15).

According to Ruether, the church always finds itself in a dialectic tension between being an established historical institution and a spirit-filled community which works on its constant renewal. While the establishment of the church as a static historical institution in the past has often meant the establishment of male power structures from which women were excluded, there have been alternative traditions of spirit-filled communities, like, for example, Montanists or Quakers, in which women participated more fully. Ruether therefore argues that Women-Church needs to reclaim these alternative traditions which have often been excluded or declared heretical by the established church in their history. She uses a review of the history of the church as a means to show how this dialectic tension has always existed within the church. Ruether criticizes the church for its one-sided focus on itself as a divinely justified institution, which she calls 'sacramental materialism' by which the work of the Holy Spirit as one of constant renewal is quenched.

> The error of historical institutions lies in their attempt to make false claims of
> spiritual efficacy for purely institutional forms of mediation of words, symbols,
> and rituals. The institutional church tries to make itself the cause of grace and

> the means of dispensing the Spirit, rather than simply being the occasion and
> context where these may take place. It institutionalizes forms of communicating
> religious meaning, and it pretends that these are the only valid channels of grace
> (Ruether 1988: 32).

However, rather than abandoning institutional structures altogether because of
their potential for abuse, Ruether argues for creatively using them and thereby
developing their potential for transformation.

Within an open framework of feminist ecclesiology it is not necessary to
decide whether structures of ordained ministry ought to be retained or
rejected. Ultimately, this is not the question. The issue is much wider: what
are the means and what are the criteria that enable different communities
which are committed to being church to transform and move beyond
kyriarchy and clericalism into an open space in which women and men can
flourish. In most churches, structures of ordained ministry, whether episcopal
or not, exist. In an increasing number of churches women are given at least
restricted access to these structures by the churches recognizing their vocations (often though within the restriction of canon law). My own denomination, the Church of England, proclaims belief in the threefold ordering of
the ordained ministry into bishops, priests and deacons. Traditionally this is
understood as a means of showing the diversity of offices and ministries rather
than as a career path. It can be read in a relational rather than a hierarchical
way. The current praxis of the Church of England, however, seems to suggest
otherwise. The threefold order of ministry is in fact divided into those orders
that women whose vocation the church recognizes can obtain and those that
they cannot. In the Church of England, women have been ordained to the
diaconate since 1987 and to the priesthood since 1994. At present, women are
barred from exercising episcopal ministry in the Church of England. In fact,
the ordination of women seems to have obtained a status of enabling the
Church of England to be divided which not even major doctrinal issues seem
to have. Those congregations that object to women exercising their ministry
within their bounds are able to receive 'alternative episcopal oversight'; they
can choose, with the permission of their diocesan bishop, to opt out of the
oversight of their regular diocesan bishop and be under the pastoral care of a
Provincial Episcopal Visitor who has not 'tainted his hands' by ordaining
women. Measures such as these show a worrying trend within a denomination
which normally prides itself on the breadth of views it encompasses.

The question I want to ask first is: what is ordained ministry and what, if
any, is its creative and constructive potential within established and non-
established churches? What difference does it make to a church if women and

men minister together? With regard to the latter, the burden should not be on women alone to transform the church or even to be content with having received access to what used to be a male domain, but it should be a chance for all people, women and men, lay and ordained, to reflect on their whole existence, every aspect of their lives, and not least their sexuality, to be part of their calling within the church. The problem of the ordination of women is not a question of employment rights, but rather a question of the church living up to its calling to enable all people to be human in the image of the Triune God and to provide space for human beings to develop the full potential of their humanity and enable others to do the same.

The ordination of women, in fact any ordination, needs to be considered in the context of the question of what it means to be church. Does ordaining anyone, creating a distinction between different ministries, enable or hinder the life of the church and all people within it? John Wijngaards, a former Roman-Catholic priest, who resigned his orders in response to the Vatican's treatment of the proponents of women's ordination in the Roman Catholic Church, describes the demand for women's ordination as being at the heart of the Catholic faith. He provides four reasons for this being the case:

(1)    It stems directly from the equality of men and women in Christ's universal priesthood, acquired through baptism.

(2)    It derives from the nature of the church as the People of God in which women as much as men are full and equal members.

(3)    It is implied in women's full participation in the whole sacramental order.

(4)    It is testified to in the *sense of faith* carried by Catholics who instinctively know that it is not God or Christ who bans women from the priesthood (Wijngaards 2001).

Barbara Brown Zikmund points out that the question of women's ordination in most Protestant denominations is connected with questions of women's admission to lay ministry and the question of the role of the laity and its equality with the clergy as such:

> In most mainstream denominations no progress is made towards the recognition of women clergy until women gain significant power and influence as laity. The journey begins with basic citizenship rights in the local congregation. Are women allowed to speak up in church meetings? Do women have a vote? Eventually, the issue expands to deal with questions of lay leadership. Can women serve in the vestry, the session, the office board, the church council? Can women represent their church at regional, diocesan or national meetings? Sometimes certain lay responsibilities call for 'ordination' as deacon or ruling elder. Main-

stream Protestant Churches rarely take up the question of women's ordination (as clergy to preach and lead worship) until questions of lay leadership are resolved (Zikmund 1986: 339).

From a feminist point of view, a hierarchical distinction between clergy and laity needs to be rejected. As Zikmund describes, for a variety of women in mainstream Protestant denominations, ordination is seen as a pragmatic matter of stepping up by degrees rather than as recognizing some women as having a particular vocation to a particular ministry. She asks how the church can legislate against class discrimination and racism and continue to legislate against sex without losing spiritual power (Zikmund 1986: 355).

For many women, seeing a woman at the altar or on the pulpit is an empowering sign of their own being church:

> I continue to feel excluded from liturgy which uses all masculine images of God, especially when there is not a woman priest at the altar. I had the wonderful experience of having a female priest for two years and it changed my worship experience and my life. I was represented and welcomed at the altar as never before or since (Winter *et al.* 1994: 16).

An obvious problem for women feeling a vocation to ordained ministry is the lack of role models. Many women resort to imitating male styles of leadership and thereby becoming token males. Within a framework of feminist ecclesiology which sees women as being church as who they are, this is not acceptable. In her keynote speech at the 2001 Women's Ordination Worldwide conference in Dublin, Rose Hudson-Wilkin said:

> Women, when we get there, we are not going to be the clones of male priests. We are going to be ourselves and we are going to make our offering according to the gifts that God has given to us. What has caused me some pain as well is to see intelligent women buying into the myth that women cannot be priests because of some 'accident of birth'—even those themselves who hold high office or are in one of the many professions which once barred them from that position. If we are saying it, then why do we expect the men to be different? (Hudson-Wilkin 2001).

Letty Russell, writing about feminist ecclesiology from her experience as a pastor in East Harlem, New York, describes women's vocation to the ordained ministry as a possibility to subvert the church into being the church. This raises two questions: what impact has the fact that women and men are ministering together had on those denominations which have admitted women to the ordained ministry? and: can the burden of transforming and subverting the church really be left to women alone? I am asking: are churches which ordain women different from those which do not? Are they by virtue of doing so any closer to a feminist vision of being church? One way to achieve transformation from within is the so-called 'march through the institutions', the gradual infiltration of the power centres of institutions such as the church by those with a different vision. For women and men with a feminist vision, this may mean to enter hierarchical structures in order to subvert them and to break them down.

What impact does the admission of women to the ordained ministry in particular denominations have on the lives of all women in those denominations? Is the ordination of women into certain offices merely a response to pragmatic necessities such as the dire shortage of priests in the Roman Catholic Church, which has led to a large number of priestless parishes being pastored by nuns, or the absence of male clergy serving at the front during the Second World War, which led the Confessing Church to ordain women pastors who were later denied their ordination rights? Mark Chaves in his study on the symbolic impact of women's ordination in American churches points out that admitting women to some or all ordained offices in a given denomination does not necessarily imply a feminist vision of gender equality:

> As such, a denomination's policy on women clergy has become an important part of its public identity, signaling to the world the denomination's location vis-à-vis certain cultural boundaries. A denomination's policy allowing (or prohibiting) women's ordination is better understood as a symbolic display of support for gender equality (or of resistance to gender equality) than as a policy either motivated by or intended to regulate the everyday reality of women inside the organization. Formal denominational policy regarding women's ordination…has a symbolic significance that is not reducible to pragmatic internal operations of the organization (Chaves 1997: 6).

Chaves points out that it is hardly ever the vision of women's equality rooted in the Christian tradition as a whole and at times in the history and theology of particular traditions which drives particular denominations to change their policy with regard to women in the ordained ministry. He highlights the impact of external pressures such as state legislation on gender equality or the women's movement as well as ecumenical relations with other denominations on such decisions. He concludes:

> …rules about women's ordination largely serve as symbolic display to the outside world, and they point to (or away from) a broader liberal agenda associated with modernity and religious accommodation to the spirit of the age. From this perspective, a denomination's formal policy about women's ordination is less an indicator of women's literal status within the denomination and more an enactment of its position vis-à-vis the liberal and modern agenda of institutionalizing individual rights. Women's ordination is about something more than females in religious leadership (Chaves 1997: 192).

In the context of this discussion of feminist ecclesiology, the question is not whether or not women ought to be ordained. The arguments and the history of various movements for the ordination of women are amply documented elsewhere. What is at issue here is whether the fundamental distinction between the ordained and the laity, which large parts of the Christian Church maintain, can still be meaningful as part of a vision of feminist ways of being church. One of the shortfalls of feminist theology and feminist ecclesiology in particular has been that its focus has been on those women's discourses of faith which maintain a liberal feminist agenda. A feminist ecclesiology which asserts that women are church, however, has to take into account all women's discourses of faith whether they subscribe to certain tenets of a feminist agenda such as women's equality or women's ordination or not. This includes movements such as the UK group Women Against the Ordination of Women. Their agenda needs to be critically and constructively evaluated along with a variety of others, as the aim of feminist ecclesiology is the liberation of *all* women and the listening of all women to each other and within the patriarchal church. One of the key characteristics of feminist ecclesiology is its pragmatic stance towards existing structures and the development of new structures. As feminist ecclesiology does not seek to develop an ideal model of being church but rather characteristics of a vision of a liberated and liberating church which can function in a variety of different structures, the question about ordination in the context of a feminist ecclesiological vision cannot be decided with an ultimate yes or no. Feminist ecclesiology counters women's deprivation of power and full citizenship in whichever form it occurs in the patriarchal church. It therefore opposes clerical structures of exploitation. At the same time, feminist ecclesiology advocates the recognition of all vocations and gifts within the church. We therefore have to recognize the subversive potential of entering the ordained ministry and of being able to lead a church of women and men into being part of the new liberated humanity. One has to ask if an ordained ministry helps or hinders women's discourses of faith. Does it create a clerical elite culture or does it provide a means for providing spaces for women's discourses of faith as part of the life of the church as a whole? On a deeper symbolic level, one has to identify the social symbolic ordering of gender-power relation with the distinction between clergy and laity and assess the practical implications this has for the life of the church.

A feminist reconception of ecclesiology which retains a concept of ordained ministry as a possibility has to emphasize the importance of a functional approach to understanding the significance of that specific ministry. Feminist ecclesiology asserts a vision of radical equality and democracy within the

church. This means that all members of the church are called and in fact
'ordained' to a ministry through their baptism, the sacramental symbol of that
vision of radical equality and democracy. The need for leadership is therefore a
merely pragmatic one: if the need is felt by a particular community, a certain
person can be commissioned to do specific ministries such as preaching or
celebrating the sacraments. This commissioning does, however, not evoke a
change in status. All authority in the *ekklesia*, the community of full citizens, is
shared authority in order to achieve the purpose of the community as a whole.
In a community in which authority is shared, the primary ministry of all
members, ordained or not, is to be 'midwives of justice' (Hess 1998), the
transformation of barriers of otherness into a celebration of difference.
Feminist ecclesiology does not primarily focus on the elite knowledge of
'doctors of the church', but rather on the practical wisdom of such midwives
of justice of which the patriarchal church has traditionally been highly
suspicious. It recognizes that at the heart of being church is not so much
orthodoxy, the right formulation of particular doctrines, not even a mis-
understood concept of 'ortho-praxy', the (morally) right doing, but the particular lives of those around the table locally and worldwide. The agenda is set
by those who suffer from lack of employment rights, from violence, from
unjust distribution of resources, from diseases such as HIV/AIDS, from
prejudice and persecution because of race or sexual orientation. It is set by the
celebration of all as human beings in the image of God and by the creation of
human dignity and justice in conversation with each other. Midwives are not
only those who help to give birth, but are traditionally also those with a
knowledge of healing, often with means rejected by conventional medicine.
Healing is the restoration of wholeness within the body, within the community as a whole.

Letty Russell and others suggest the round table as the image for the use of
authority in a liberated community. The round table allows no distinction
between ranks or people of different status. It shows that any ministry of
proclaiming the gospel in a particular community is rooted in listening, in
hearing into speech. Likewise, any celebration of the sacraments with and on
behalf of the whole community is rooted in the celebration of the embodied
lives of each and every member of the community rather than in the
celebrant's symbolizing Christ. A concept of authority shared around the table
is diametrically opposed to the language of headship, the distinction between
Christ as head (represented by a [male] leader) and the church as body, as well
as the language of pastor and sheep. It is a concept of ecclesial agency of all
members of the church. Shared authority enables all members of a com-

munity to break cycles of oppression and secrecy, to name their joys and sufferings and to be open to each other and to the whole of creation. It is important not to see shared authority as an ideal, but to recognize it in its sometime harsh and painful reality, having to listen to unpopular opinions, transparency in financial matters, and so on. It means that everyone has the power to name the agenda, that hidden agendas are brought out in the open and listened to by everyone. It requires the ability to develop constructive approaches to the resolution of conflict rather than executive decisions which sweep potentially difficult situations under the carpet. Sharing authority in community means being church in the image of the Triune God, participating in God's openness to the world. This sharing of power and openness can work with or without designated or even ordained ministers. Different communities have opted for different ways of doing this. While the Women-Church movement rejects the ordination of women and in fact the creation of any parallel church structures as a primary goal, the St Hilda community did employ a community priest while also celebrating the Eucharist together when no priest was available. The clandestine ordination of women to the Roman Catholic priesthood by a bishop of the underground Roman Catholic Church (and its subsequent being ignored by the Vatican) are as much part of the history of women's being church as the stories of women who have suffered abuse at the hands of male clergy and in fact the stories of women who often late in life did see their vocation recognized by the institutional church.

A significant number of those fighting for the ordination of women do not describe themselves as feminist. The contribution which feminist ecclesiology can make to the debate about the ordination of women is to highlight the fact that the question of women's ordination needs to be discussed in a wider context of what it means to be church. This is a conscious move away from the framework in which many of the opponents to women's ordination locate their opposition, the question whether or not a particular denomination has the 'right' to admit women to the priesthood or even the episcopate, while others, such as the Roman Catholic Church or the churches of the Christian East, do not do so. It places the debate about ordination in the context of an ecclesiology which challenges the church into being the full church of God and of all human beings in the image of the divine, regardless of particular man-made and male-dominated structures.

# Chapter Six

# Celebrating Embodiment:
# Towards a Feminist Sacramental Ecclesiology

According to traditional understandings of the church, the life of the church centres around the preaching of the word and sacramental praxis. Martin Luther and other reformers, as well as the Thirty-Nine Articles of the Church of England, define the church as the place where the word of God is preached and the sacraments are celebrated accordingly. Christ is present in the church in both word and sacrament and the church manifests itself where the word of Scripture is read and the sacraments are celebrated. For a feminist rereading of ecclesiology and of the life of the church, it is therefore necessary to focus on both proclamation of the word and sacramental praxis as essential for the nature of the church. Sacramentality is of particular importance for our feminist project of reinterpretation, as the reality of sacramental praxis points to the fact that the experience of being church and essentially the experience of Christ in the church is an experience which is the embodiment of the word, but goes beyond the word and includes all aspects of human life and human bodily experience. In addition, the reality of women being confined to mere recipients of the sacraments by their exclusion from the celebration of the Eucharist can still be seen as one of the most powerful manifestations of the attitude the patriarchal church has to women:

> In sacramental life, all the symbols of the life of the community, as a life grounded in the divine and experienced together, are alienated from the people and made into magic tools possessed by the clergy through an ordination that comes from 'above' (Ruether 1988: 77).

Denise Lardner Carmody urges feminist theologians to affirm and to reconsider the centrality of the sacraments and sacramentality. She accuses the church of living in permanent sin against women if it continues to exclude women from large parts of its sacramental praxis and thereby from the dynamic centre of its life:

> To say the least, it is a great irony that women have seldom been ordained as priests, asked to officiate ministerially at the altar to confect the sacraments, administer the liturgical rites that materialize grace. To say what is necessary, it is a scandal, a great revelation of sin. Without becoming anachronistic, and so asking earlier times to display later sensitivities, we still have to say that so to exclude from priestly ministry women, the sex who carry physical life, incarnate spirituality, directly within them, the sex whose hands have often patted and poked new life into its first squalling overture, betrays a stunning ignorance of the Incarnation (Carmody 1995: 126).

She therefore urges women not to miss out on the materialization of divine grace in the form of the sacraments: 'Until we have figured out how the sacraments are acts of Christ fully appropriate to our cause of realizing in all ways the equality of women with men in the possession of humanity, we feminists have missed a great opportunity, overlooked a key citadel or territory we must gain' (Carmody 1995: 126). In her work on the sacramental and especially the eucharistic piety of mediaeval women as a possible source for the construction of a feminist theology of the Eucharist, Joy A. Schroeder writes: 'I would contend, however, that to abandon the richness of the sacramental life to the "men's church" is to deny oneself the same sacraments that our foremothers fought to receive' (Schroeder 1991: 226). On a similar line Mary Collins argues:

> The Roman Catholic eucharistic heritage is a rich, dense source of meaning and power for women. That meaning and power does not all lie in the past; it has a present and future for those who trust themselves to eucharistic action in troubled times. To insist upon construing eucharist solely as a symbol of male power is to squander a known source of spiritual vitality in the Catholic community (Collins 1991: 11).

Susan A. Ross hopes to bring feminist and sacramental theology, so vital to Roman Catholic theology and ecclesiology, into a dialogue which could be fruitful for both. Feminism and especially feminist theology poses a 'sacramental critique' to the tradition of Roman Catholic sacramental theology by challenging some of its main presuppositions (Ross 1993, 1998). She criticizes sacramental theologians, even though an interest in the equality of women can be noted in at least some of them, for not taking into account the experiences of women. These can only be detected by a theological anthropology which lays bare the ambivalence attributed to the body in traditional theology. Feminist theology needs to reconsider the sacraments even though they have in the past represented the alienation of women from the church. In addition, some of the central symbolism which is important for sacramental theology not only does not take into account the experience of women, but also assigns women a particular, essentially subordinate place within the church. The connection between feminist theology and sacramental theology is the significance of the body and embodiment for both of them. Ross sees it as the purpose of her work on sacraments to show 'how the implications of embodiment inform sacramental theology both critically and constructively' (Ross 1989). Ross uses a re-established sacramental theology as the theological means by which women's bodies and experiences can be affirmed as sacred. Feminist theology, uncomfortable with fixed and absolute categories such as a canon of sacraments or the debate about the 'validity' of a sacrament, seeks a sacramental theology which is grounded in the lives of the women and men who are church and in the being-in-relation of the Triune God, manifested in God's extravagant self-giving in creation and incarnation. Feminist sacramental theology, according to Ross, has to be able to face the ambiguity inherent in the complexity and fluidity of all human experience. Developing Ross's thoughts further, I would argue that such ambiguity is inherent in a feminist understanding of church as a space of bounded openness itself.

The most important aspect of Ross's theological anthropology of the body is her reinterpretation of sexual difference. For Ross, the difference between sacramental theology and feminist theology lies, on the side of traditional sacramental theology, in its interpretation of sexual difference as an essentialist and dichotomist gender binary, and on the side of feminism, in an understanding of sexual difference as 'differentiation'. Such an understanding of differentiation enables a multiplicity of sacramental experiences and consequently a multivalence of the symbols involved which is vital for a project like the feminist ecclesiology I advocate in this book. Ross calls for an increased sensitivity to the symbols used in sacramental theology, and for the exploration of gender as an 'unacknowledged dimension' of that symbolic expression.

In addition, Ross, like Ruether, calls for the sacramental praxis of the church to be rooted in the practice of social justice, unlike a sacramental theology and praxis which neither involves nor represents women and their experience. Ross's most important contribution to the feminist discussion of sacramental theology is to re-establish the essential connection between sacramental theology and the incarnation as the central christological point. According to Ross, our understanding of the incarnation cannot be based on an essentialist understanding of the maleness of Christ, but has to affirm that it was in fact humanity that the divine assumed. This renders invalid the notion of sex complementarity as the gender construction which is inherent to traditional sacramental theology, and enables a multiplicity of understandings to be represented in sacramental theology.

Susan Ross's primary theological interest lies in the spelling out of the significance and inevitability of the connection between theological anthropology and sacramental theology of which feminist theology makes us aware. Ross, however, does not make the connection between anthropology, sacramental theology and ecclesiology. Her understanding of theological anthropology as vital for the interpretation of sacraments remains at the level of the individual human being. As important as her reconception of the body self and subject is for her critique of the sacramental theology and praxis of the church, she does not go as far as re-establishing sacraments as symbols which are experienced in the community and in fact provide the vital connection between the individual and the community. The significance of sacraments and sacramentality for this reconstruction of ecclesiology lies in my understanding of sacramental celebration as the embodied interaction between the individual, the divine and the community. Such interaction cannot be without the sexual dimension inherent to being human. It is here, at this dynamic centre of ecclesial life, that women manifest themselves as church and thereby embody the being-in-relation of the Triune God creative and incarnate. Sacramental celebration is the enactment of Christ's presence in the church as the body of Christ manifested in women's and men's bodies. They connect the major stages of human lives with the life of the church as the body of Christ and are celebrations of God's presence in the lives of human beings. If feminist ecclesiology is the theological description of women being church, women have to reconsider not only the significance, but also the contents of sacramental celebration within the church.

If sacraments are enactments of Christ's presence at crucial stages in the course of life, then we have to ask whether the inherited sacramental canon of the church fits the crucial events in a woman's life or if it is based on the assumption of a church dominated by male human beings. In sacramental celebration, the mutual administration of Christ's presence in which being church is realized, women who are church become Christlike for each other. This means to deny the argument that the male priest has to resemble Christ physically, and to deny the nuptial structure of reality between Christ and the church and replace it with a feminist sacramental ecclesiology in which the church is the space where human beings, as particular sexual human beings, make Christ's presence real for each other. Such Christlikeness can no longer be gendered; in other words: we cannot restrict ourselves to attributing some aspects of Christlikeness to men and others to women, such as attributing

Christlike authority and leadership to men and Christlike submission, obedience and servanthood to women. Being Christlike to each other means that both men and women represent Christ's presence to each other in each and every aspect of the embodied reality of the church.

After these general reflections on the possibility of a feminist reconsideration of sacramental ecclesiology, I now want to take a closer look at some of the particular sacraments which are used in the praxis of the Christian Church. For the purpose of this book, I would like to restrict myself to the sacraments of baptism and Eucharist as they are recognized as sacramental acts by the majority of Christian Churches. I want to look at what these sacramental acts signify for the life of the church and those who participate in them, both as recipients and as those who dispense them on behalf of the church. Both baptism and the Eucharist can be read as symbols too powerful to give up, but must be reread in the wider context of an ecclesiology which affirms the sacredness of women's embodied lives and experiences and is therefore ready to open up the canon of sacramental acts and rites to include other forms of celebration which identify and sanctify significant stages of women's lives.

Baptism, as understood in the praxis of the Early Church, communicates a fundamental message of equality among those who receive it, as well as those who baptize. Unlike the Jewish rite of circumcision, baptism is a rite of initiation open to anyone, male or female, Jew or Gentile, and in fact renders those distinctions insignificant. There is also evidence that in the earliest days, women were baptized by women and men by men (due to the fact that everyone was baptized naked), a praxis still retained in the church's statement that anyone, ordained or not, can baptize, at least in situations of emergency when no member of the ordained clergy is available.

I must, however, go deeper and ask what the rite of baptism actually signifies and whether those meanings can actually be retained in the context of a feminist reconsideration of the Christian Church. In this context, I would like to suggest a reconsideration of baptism which rather assumes the praxis of infant baptism that is common in some, though not all, Christian Churches. The praxis of baptizing committed adult believers would need a different set of reconsiderations. What follows is to be understood as a case study, not as the only feminist ecclesiological reconsideration of baptism.

Baptism is a rite of initiation into the Christian community, an act of welcome, but there are also elements of purification. It is regarded as an act of new birth, in addition to and essentially superseding the natural birth as a result of sexual intercourse and therefore tainted with original sin. This taint has often been associated with the female involvement in giving birth, most importantly the female blood shed in menstruation and childbirth. In the Mediaeval Church, due to high rates of infant mortality, children were to be baptized as soon as possible after birth, as baptism was regarded necessary for salvation. This meant that, in most cases, mothers did not attend their children's baptisms as they were still excluded from attending church due to the period of purification imposed on them after childbirth. This affirms the separation of a child's natural birth and the new birth signified in baptism. Christine Gudorf identifies sacraments as male substitutions for things that women do naturally and calls for a reconnection of these male rites of substitution with the natural female acts that they signify (Gudorf 1987). Feminist theologians have been highly critical of the concept of original sin as it denies the natural goodness of all human life in the image of the divine and as the impurity it asserts is largely connected to female involvement in sexual intercourse. A feminist ecclesiology that seeks to reconsider baptism as a rite of initiation therefore needs to ask whether an understanding of baptism as washing away original sin can indeed be an appropriate act of welcome of a human being, infant or adult, into a church which celebrates the goodness of all human life and of female sexuality in particular.

Much feminist criticism has also been extended to the Trinitarian baptismal formula which only recognizes baptism as valid if it is done in the name of the Father, Son and Holy Spirit. Does this mean that baptism is only valid if it is understood as baptism into a male-defined church identified by its relationship with a God that can only be spoken about in terms of a male Trinity? Or is a rereading of the Trinitarian formula possible as divine being in relation, which could also be seen as God, for example, Mother, Lover and Friend?

Feminist ecclesiology has also hitherto been done largely in a context of adult commitment to a community of faith rather than understanding the church as something into which one is received as an infant without being given a choice. Therefore serious questions of a praxis of infant baptism arise. If baptism is interpreted as a rite of spiritual rebirth which supersedes the natural birth by a woman mother, I want to ask whether this adds to the denial of relationships such as between mother and daughter which is hardly mentioned at all in the Christian tradition.

Catherine Mowry LaCugna, in her seminal work on the Trinity, highlights some of the possibilities of rethinking baptism in a Trinitarian formula which are useful for a feminist reconsideration of the church (LaCugna 1991). She contrasts separate and personal being with divine being in communion. Through baptism, a human being is received into the divine being in communion and thereby into communion with others: into the church.

Finally, I want to ask whether baptism as it is practised focuses on the child rather than on the child in relation with her/his parents and essentially with her/his mother. There are two aspects to this question: first of all, does the equality which is conveyed through baptism as a rite for everyone leave enough room for differences between human beings, that is, how can a baptism for a girl be made special as the reception of a female child whose emerging sexual being is valued and celebrated as a member of the church? And, secondly, where does that leave the mother who has just undergone one of the most traumatic experiences of her life in giving birth? How can her part in the emergence of this new life and her change of status as mother be affirmed and celebrated in the context of Christian initiation?

With regard to the latter, the Christian tradition does provide a (now rather marginalized) rite for women who have just given birth, the rite of churching. In order to rethink this rite, it is, however, necessary to purge this rite and its traditions from any unnecessary and harmful connotations of purification from ritual and bodily impurity which it assigns to childbirth. The Mediaeval Church listed the rite of churching among the 'sacramentals', rites which were not sacraments as such, but had a dimension of the sacramental. This is interesting as it seems to hint at a connection between women's giving birth and the reality of the sacred, which has nevertheless been distorted into the realm of ritual impurity, perhaps as a result of male fear of the proximity of women's sexuality to the very processes of life and death. The 'Book of Common Prayer' describes 'churching' as a rite of thanksgiving after childbirth and it is this positive aspect which can be a starting point for our reconsideration. Joanne M. Pierce lists five layers of meaning for the rite of churching in its traditional form:

(1) purification (blood pollution or sexual pleasure);
(2) repentance (forgiveness/reconciliation; connected with purification);
(3) blessing (connected with reconciliation and celebration);
(4) thanksgiving (for a safe delivery/survival of childbirth);
(5) celebration (private/social/official) (Pierce 1999).

From a feminist point of view, it almost goes without saying that the rite of churching cannot be reintroduced as such, but what is important here is the fact that such a rite does in fact exist and some of the aspects of its meaning may in fact be lost and in need of recovery in the context of a feminist reconsideration of ecclesiology and sacramental celebration. Pierce's list of layers of meaning of the rite of churching points to the complexity of the kind of rite which could be meaningful in the context of Women-Church. What is required is a reconsideration of the praxis of sacramental initiation as a whole which involves both mother and child and recognizes their relationship both on a personal level and in the context of the church community as a whole. Worship in the context of Women-Church is only meaningful if it is embodied and recognizes both the public and the personal dimension as well as their inherent connection. A further question is that of other significant adults involved in the parenting and raising of the child. These include fathers, or in the case of same-sex couples parenting a child, the role of the other partner (as well as in the case of gay couples, the relationship between the birth mother and the couple raising the child). In this context, the role of godparents also needs to be reconsidered.

The starting point of a reconsideration of sacramental initiation which involves the mother as well as the child should be the experience that the mother has just undergone, that of pregnancy and giving birth. Despite the achievements of modern medicine, these are still deeply traumatic for the mother. Pregnancy, even if desired and welcomed, is a deeply painful and emotionally involving experience for the mother. Her body is for the period of the pregnancy inhabited by another human being. This is followed by what is again a painful experience of separation, which the mother often experiences as total loneliness and desertion. To be meaningful the rite has to recognize these experiences for what they are. In addition, the expectations placed on the mother by her immediate environment and the wider society need to be recognized and taken into account. This may be the place where elements of purification and reconciliation could come into consideration. What needs to be rejected are of course not notions of ritual or any other form of sexual impurity, but a rejection of the physical reality of pregnancy, giving birth and emotional suffering. Then the rite can move on to welcoming both mother and child into the community. The mother will never be the same again; she does not re-enter the community as the person she was but in her new role and responsibility as a mother who cares for a child and bears the primary responsibility for the child to grow from dependency into a person in her/his own right. This cannot be a solitary process but one for which the mother and the child, as well as any other significant adults involved, need the prayers and the support of the whole community. A rite of Christian initiation which involves both mother and child acknowledges this responsibility and celebrates the goodness of new life having come into the world. A number of recent baptismal rites include prayers for the parents and godparents. These, however, often appear at the end of the rite and seem to be added on, rather than an integral part of the rite.

I want to recognize that in the context of traditional faith communities and institutional churches, baptism is still initiation into fundamental ambiguity. Even if baptism itself signifies equality among women and men in Christ, the reality and praxis of most ecclesial communities seems to suggest otherwise. Susan Roll asks:

> How would responsible, honest prebaptismal catechesis for prospective Christians deal with the inherent ambivalence in Christian tradition and formal doctrine toward women's equal human dignity and human rights? How would credible catechesis reconcile the split between, for example, visionary statements such as Gal. 3.28 and the essentialist perspective on women and men's nature embodied in, among other sources, *Mulieris Dignitatem* of John Paul II which identifies women's very being with specific functions such as mother or virgin? (Roll 2000: 308).

This raises the question: what does baptism communicate and does baptism indeed provide a challenge to the church which it needs to learn to live up to?

Two further issues are to be considered here: the role of the minister in the context of such a renewed and integrated form of Christian initiation and the space in which such a rite of initiation should take place.

Susan Roll points out that women have often experienced it as alienating that they had to undergo a rite of churching performed by a male priest. She highlights 'the underlying mentality that women are functionally objects, not acting subjects of their own experience and of the religious rituals which set their lived experience into a meaning-framework of divinity and eternity' (Roll 2000). As I have argued in the previous chapter on the reclaiming of Christian ministry as mutual agency rather than as pastoral and ritual activity in a subject-object framework, I want to ask the question: who ministers to whom in the rite of Christian initiation for mother and child? Feminist ecclesiology essentially seeks to subvert and break the binary understanding of ministry as performed by a (male) subject (or even a female assuming a male-defined role) to a (female) object. Christian initiation is a rite performed by the whole of the Christian community of which mother and child are integral parts. While the child cannot speak for her/himself, the mother certainly can and should be regarded as giving herself and her experiences to the whole community to be recognized as not only her private experiences which need to be covered up, but as a political experience which takes place in the political and social context of the whole community by which it is, after all, shaped. While the minister, be it a priest or someone else, may act as a representative of the wider church, this ministry needs to be seen in the wider context of the community which is represented not only by her/him, but also by other significant adults (and children) who represent the community as a whole in their relationship with the mother and her child. Traditionally, a woman who went for her churching was accompanied by female friends and her midwife, often women who shared their own similar experiences with the new mother. They not only accompanied the mother to be ritually churched but also participated in subsequent celebrations. A revised rite of Christian initiation which combines the baptism of the child with an acknowledgment of the experiences of the mother, as well as other significant adults who assume a new role in the life of the growing child, needs to recognize these persons as participating ministers who represent the life and experience of the wider church. Susan Roll writes:

> The advent of women as agents of liturgy who are learning to speak in their own voice and identify their own experience, offers the possibility to transform ritual and public prayer in a more wholistic [sic] and authentic direction. In the case of childbearing, a profound life-experience of many but not all women, it is new mothers themselves who are in the best position to testify to the dynamics and presence of God in their pregnancy and birthing—and to invite their faith communities to rejoice with them (Roll 2000: 303).

Secondly, I want to reconsider the space and context in which Christian initiation takes place. Susan Roll mentions that some of those who call for a renewal of churching in its traditional form want to see it as a 'ritual form of witness against abortion' (Roll 2000: 316). This points to a grave distortion of what such an affirmation of motherhood as part of a new child's life could mean. It has to be taken into account that in modern Western society the heterosexual nuclear family is no longer the only context in which children are born and raised. The mother is also not the only person who will be involved in raising the child. Christian initiation needs to take account of the particular context in which this particular child is born and will live. Despite the availability of contraceptives, pregnancy and childbirth do not always happen by choice. In addition, the physical context in which such a rite takes place also needs to be considered. Baptism and churching traditionally took place in the actual church building. While this again reflects the public nature of Christian worship and the entering or re-entering of that public space, it is often not the only significant space for those seeking Christian initiation. As for baptism, in danger of death of mother or child immediately following childbirth, baptisms have and are certainly being performed in other spaces such as hospitals or even homes. Yet a feminist ecclesiology that recognizes and affirms the presence of the sacred in the whole world needs to recognize the significance of such other spaces not only in the context of emergency and imminent death.

One possibility would certainly be for a ceremony of initiation to begin in the home or even the hospital, the location where the birth took place or the space in which the life of parents and child are primarily situated, and from there to move to a space occupied by the wider community to symbolize the connection between personal and public, secular and sacred in the emerging new relationship.

The second of those rites regarded as primary sacraments by the Christian Churches is the celebration of a meal in memory of Christ's death and resurrection as well as in anticipation of the eschatological fellowship of all believers with Christ in his coming kingdom. This rite is referred to by a number of different names usually revealing something of the theology and ecclesiology of those who use them: the Eucharist, the Lord's Supper or Communion are among those terms most widely used.

The celebration of this meal has been the site of ambiguity for women throughout Christian history. While on the one hand, the sharing of bread and wine designating Christ's body and blood symbolizes the openness of Christ's table fellowship to all who wish to receive it, the Eucharist has also been an experience of exclusion for women. This does not only refer to the refusal of a number of denominations, the Roman Catholic Church or the Orthodox Churches to name the most prominent, to allow women to perform this rite and prepare the meal which is to be shared, but it also refers to conditions put on those who receive this meal such as the fact that the Orthodox Churches still advise menstruating women not to receive communion. Again, the preparation of a meal is something many women do every day. It is the fundamental expression of women's nurturing role in their families. The sharing of a meal can be one of the most empowering experiences for any community of people gathered for a specific purpose and be it only that of fellowship with each other.

The Eucharist is a meal and yet it is not. During the first centuries the breaking of bread and sharing of the cup developed from an actual meal at which food and drink were shared in memory of Christ's last sharing of bread and cup with his disciples, into a symbolic meal which had to be performed by a specific and male minister who came to be seen in the role of a priest offering a sacrifice resembling the sacrifice of Christ on Calvary. In the Middle Ages, the sacrifice of the Mass became the means by which the institutional church dispensed from its treasure of divine grace which it and it alone administered on God's behalf. The sacrificial shedding of blood through the death of Christ on the cross had to be re-enacted through the bloodless sacrifice of the Mass. Again there is the highly contentious blood symbolism here: while female blood flows uncontrolled in menstruation and childbirth and is regarded as polluting, purification is required through the controlled shedding of blood in the sacrifice which is enacted by men as a symbolic act of identification and belonging (Jay 1985 and 1992). The interpretation of the death of Christ as sacrificial and substitutionary atonement in itself is contentious for feminist theologians. Yet what is at issue here is again the question if and why the natural process of preparing and sharing of food needs to be superseded by a male-defined symbolic, substitutionary and sacrificial meal.

In her poem 'Questions of a Reading Christian Woman', Carola Moosbach, a feminist poet, asks:

> Who baked the bread where were
> the women disciples and who set the table
> at that last and first Lord's Supper
> Who washed whose feet then did the men
> also serve women and why and when
> did they stop doing that why is a man's blood
> precious that of a woman however impure what made
> the Eucharist bony and shallow how can we
> begin to taste God's love anew and be satisfied
> through sharing? (Moosbach 2002: 103).

These are essentially the questions at stake for a reconsideration of the Eucharist in the context of feminist ecclesiology. Whether or not celebrations of shared meals as part of feminist liturgies should be regarded as women claiming the power to celebrate communion, even though it was denied to them by church authorities, was an open question among the first women of the Women-Church movement. Should women ask for the right to participate in the celebration of what essentially remained a male-defined rite? Or was the Eucharist as the most powerful focus of the church's life and message too important to be left to the male institutional church alone?

A further question to be considered here is that of the ambiguous relationship between women and food in general. Food is not only prepared by women to be shared and as a means of nurturing others, but is also connected with the prevailing problem of eating disorders connected with women's desperate attempt to conform to standards of society and attempted denial of their emerging sexuality. Caroline Walker Bynum's research into the eucharistic spirituality of mediaeval religious women shows that women often fasted excessively and refused any food intake other than the Eucharist in order to achieve the absence of menstruation as a sign of their female sexuality (Bynum 1987). In the contemporary world, women are under constant pressure to diet. Melissa Raphael describes women succumbing to this pressure which is also often prevalent in religious circles: '...women who diet are compensating for that exclusion [i.e. from the sacred] in their attempt to emulate the changeless perfection of the body' (Raphael 1996: 101). Later on, she points out that with regard to food women are in a no-win situation:

> Whether a woman 'starves' her children by becoming fat herself or whether she fattens them into a state of (social) vulnerability, her feeding is liable to put her in the wrong; it is in danger of profaning her and her offspring (Raphael 1996: 102).

How can a meal, symbolic or actual, be a symbol of empowering and celebrating women's bodies and sexualities if society and the church itself send out such conflicting messages? And yet the Eucharist is at the heart of the Christian Church and can therefore not be surrendered lightly.

What is needed here is an enquiry into the multivalent symbolism of the eucharistic celebration in order to achieve, if this is indeed a desirable outcome, a feminist reinterpretation. Is the Eucharist really only the Lord's Supper or does it also symbolize and enact communion, the sharing of food, but also of the very lives of individual believers, of the whole church community and essentially of the shared divine being in communion? The Eucharist is essentially communion with each other and communion with the divine; it is participation in the life of the whole church from which no one is excluded, and participation in the life of the Triune God. From a feminist perspective I would want to understand communion, however, not as something that takes place between human beings and God or between human beings alone, but essentially between God and the whole of creation. The celebration of communion is essentially the celebration of the earth community as a whole. Being church can only be meaningful if it is tied in with responsible praxis and embodied awareness for both the creator and the whole of creation. In her book *Gaia and God*, Rosemary Radford Ruether sees the Christian sacramental tradition as one of the potential resources for desperately required earth healing (Ruether 1993b). As such, it is a celebration of the goodness of embodiment, a celebration of divine embodiment through the incarnation and of the embodiment of the church in the bodies and lives of women and men who are church.

Any praxis or theology of exclusion is contrary to this powerful message which is at the heart of the Christian Church. Catherine Mowry LaCugna refers to the work of the contemporary Greek Orthodox theologian John Zizioulas, who identifies the Eucharist as 'the sacramental sign of inclusiveness (which makes the scandal even greater when the Eucharist becomes the source of division or inequity)'. She continues:

> The celebration of the Eucharist establishes a network of relationships that is
> supposed to allow persons to subsist, to be in relationship, in freedom. In the
> Christian community there should no longer be female and male, slave and free,
> Gentile and Jew, but Christ is to be all and in all. Authentic personhood is the
> catholic mode of presence in the world. The church as the body of Christ is
> itself catholic, and every baptized Christian 'is the whole Christ and the whole
> Church' (LaCugna 1991: 264).

I want to ask whether this theological description of the eucharistic celebration as the realization of communion among persons and with the whole earth community is indeed an appropriate description of the experience of women as they participate in eucharistic rites in different churches. Or is it an ideal, a reminder of what the Eucharist ought to symbolize? From a feminist perspective such an ideal which might proclaim an eschatological reality cannot be enough if the corresponding actual structures of social justice and equality are not established at the same time. This connection between embodiment, the affirmation of women's sexualities and social justice and liberation is at the heart of all feminist reconsiderations of ecclesiology, and any notion of being church which does not take these into account is rendered meaningless. We have to ask: who defines the authenticity of the eucharistic celebration? Susan Ross writes:

> My own sense is that the criterion for authentic Eucharist ought not so much to
> be location or whether there is an 'official' presider but rather to what extent the
> Eucharist 'effects what it signifies'—that is, unity, community, a sense of radical
> inclusion, a concern for feeding our many hungers and thirsts, a living out of the
> real presence of Christ in the midst of human life (Ross 1998: 194).

In other words: Women-Church Eucharist is authentic, not to the imitation of a male-defined tradition, but to those very people who are celebrating it with each other and in and for a world which needs to hear its message of radical equality and justice for all. The celebration of the Eucharist is a proclamation of the values of the reign of God which is being built by the church. Such a proclamation, however, needs to be accompanied by actions that tie in with an agenda of social justice and equality for all. Only then, a distinction between the sacred and the secular is no longer maintained. As such the Eucharist is not so much a retrospective enactment of a meal that Jesus shared with his disciples, but it is a forward-looking prototypical celebration of those values which were proclaimed by Jesus and his followers in the first century and are being proclaimed wherever women gather as church today.

Here I have to ask whether women can endorse the development from an actual to a symbolic meal, in other words whether the Eucharist as merely a symbolic meal in terms of a male substitution rite can be meaningful for women in the context of a feminist reconsideration. While on the one hand, it is important for women to reclaim those sacramental exclusion zones, I also want to ask whether the symbolic sharing of wafers and communion wine can carry the meaning of the actual embodiment of shared justice and equality that feminist reconstructions of what it means to be church seek to proclaim. A feminist celebration of communion could therefore take place in the context of a shared meal or even the sharing of food with those who do not have any, such as the homeless. Such a transformed and transforming action signifies the open invitation of God to all, which is proclaimed in the celebration of the Eucharist, and the Eucharist in turn becomes a proclamation of the church as the open community which participates in and embodies God's very being in communion.

Feminist eucharistic spirituality can therefore not be individualistically focused on receiving the body and blood of Christ, but has to focus on sharing food and drink which signifies shared participation in the life of the Triune God. Its emphasis is not on transforming the spiritual state of the individual, but on proclaiming the transformation of structures of church and society so that persons may live and be affirmed in their full personhood in the image of God.

Again, I want to ask whether this is appropriately symbolized in a Eucharist being celebrated and distributed by one minister/priest who represents both Christ and the wider church, or whether in sharing a sacramental meal those who participate in it become Christlike to each other. This could be expressed in a eucharistic prayer which is spoken by all or a number of different participants rather than only by one ordained person.

The liturgies used need to reflect the message proclaimed by the celebration. Feminist liturgical groups to a large extent depart from the established and authorized liturgies as they themselves often express the kind of exclusion that a feminist communion meal seeks to reject. None of the eucharistic prayers in the new Church of England *Common Worship* rites, for example, takes account of God-language which is not in some way or other male. Liturgy is 'the work of the people' and must therefore reflect who these people are as sexual human beings who embody the body of Christ. The issue here is *exclusive* language. That means understanding exclusive liturgical language as a symptom of an exclusion that goes much wider than just the *language* of worship. Arguments such as the resignation of David Frost, professor of English and member of the liturgical commission, over the issue of inclusive language 'based on the principle that worship of the Church should be in the language of the day, rather than of any minority or pressure-group' show exactly that misconception: women are understood as a 'minority pressure group' demanding their rights rather than as part of the body of Christ who wish the fact that they are part of the body of Christ expressed in the body of Christ's most sacred acts. Janet Morley and Hannah Ward argue:

> Exclusive language is not a trivial matter, in church or out of it. It is both an accurate symptom of women's actual extinction from many central forms of ministry and decision-making; and it is also a means of continually re-creating the attitudes which support such exclusion as 'normal' or within the purposes of God (Morley and Ward 1986: 2).

Before I can talk about constructive approaches to transforming liturgical language, I have to look at the existing texts and identify them as exclusive, as perpetuating a particular social-symbolic order that understands man's worship as normative and women as at best 'included'. This means questioning the theology that is behind certain liturgical revisions. And it certainly means for women to make clear that they are church and therefore voices to be heard in worshipping God, rather than a marginalized minority that makes its presence felt. Changing a few words in a liturgy that is otherwise full of men's theology and men's prayers is not going to achieve that. And yet in claiming that women are church, pray with the church and participate in the liturgical tradition of the church, women have to do more than just go off and write their own women's liturgies. Women have to reclaim participation in the liturgy by establishing themselves as readers and 'users' of liturgical texts: a process that goes much further than the revision of words. This means asking what is signified by women participating in the celebration of the Eucharist, using the existing prayers as they are or even with token gestures of inclusivized language.

Three factors have to be taken into account for our feminist critical reading of eucharistic rites: first, I want to ask about the importance of women for the authoring process of the texts in question; secondly, I ask whether women were intended as potential readers and interpreters of these texts. This includes seeing women not only as readers and receivers, but also as authors of new meaning to be found within the existing rites. I then discover that with few exceptions, women were not present as authors of liturgical texts and also not addressed as their intended recipients. This leads to the third dimension: the texts themselves. They have to be questioned as to how they create reality and contribute to a particular social-symbolic order in which women are now accepted as presidents of the Eucharist, but only on the grounds of their acceptance of what is still very much a male-defined role. Reflecting on the texts themselves I want to ask what role women have played in the process of creating the texts themselves as well as the process of creating the meaning of the texts.

So, let us take a brief look at the eucharistic celebration in one particular tradition, that of the Church of England. The Eucharist begins by saying the Prayers of Penitence: 'Almighty God, our heavenly Father, we have sinned against you and against our fellow men... For the sake of your Son Jesus Christ...' and one almost wants to respond in a Mary Dalyesque fashion: 'If God is male, the male is God.' So what happened to women being church then? And does this mean that the God who is worshipped in the Eucharist is as inevitably male as those who celebrate the rite? Women who have been brought up with a false sense of humility might have to think twice about saying: 'We do not presume to come to this your table, merciful Lord, trusting in our own righteousness, but in your manifold and great mercies. We are not worthy so much as to gather up the crumbs under your table.' These are words put into their mouths by a male-dominated church that has declared women unworthy of representing Christ in those most holy mysteries which express the very reality of what it means to be church. The Eucharist celebrated in such a way brings home the fact that, yes, Christ does grant us 'so to eat his flesh and drink his blood', but these words are put into women's mouths by those who declared women's flesh impure and desired not to be defiled by their blood, 'that we may evermore dwell in him and he in us', Christ who chose to dwell in a woman's body, God incarnate and God's mother incarnating.

The eucharistic celebration is the intersection between God, the church and the individual. In order to do justice to all three of these dimensions, we have to read and reread the existing traditions from the perspective not of including the 'feminine dimension', but taking into account and making explicit not only that women are church, but that we would not have the flesh and blood of Christ if it had not been for a woman's flesh and a woman's blood. What is more presumptuous than anything here is the pronoun 'we' which pretends a false uniformity still based on the male as the norm worshipping a male God who supposedly transcends sex and gender and yet is worshipped in forms still highly suggestive of a patriarchal social-symbolic order. Christianity as a historical religion perceives the process of tradition not as one of passive reception and repetition, but of creative interaction with what is received and transformed over the generations by those who are church.

A choice of Eucharistic Prayers follows the Peace. These are the most central part of the eucharistic celebration, again ridden with male and masculine imagery for God: 'holy father, heavenly king, almighty and eternal God, through Jesus Christ your only Son our Lord. For he is your living word, through him you have created all things from the beginning, and formed us in your image', 'born as man...and exalted him to your right hand on high'. Such an explicit male image for God makes it difficult for women to perceive them-selves in the image of a God who exalts men, who then in turn subdue women. To perceive such worship not only as joy, but also as duty, rings painfully in the ears of women who are constantly reminded of their duty to submit to men who exalt themselves on high and grant women no more than a token position in the church. To speak of God having freed us from the slavery of sin remains an abstract concept as long as women are still slaves of men in the manifold ways that are still rife in a modern world that prides itself on the abolition of slavery. To be the people of a male God's own possession will not be understood as a concept of liberation as long as men still perceive their wives as their property. Such imagery will remain abstract rather than rooted in the particular realities from which it is supposedly taken and will therefore be contrary to the concrete reality of the incarnation through a woman's body which is at the heart of the eucharistic celebration. Images of relationships based on property and possession are not expressions of the liberating reality of women being church as long as they are modelled on realities in real life which are destructive for women.

In a similar way, the Eucharist is perceived as remembering the one perfect sacrifice:

> Therefore, heavenly Father, we remember his offering of himself made once for all upon the cross, and proclaim his mighty resurrection and glorious ascension. As we look for his coming in glory, we celebrate with this bread and this cup his one perfect sacrifice.

And yet it is the reality of many cultures that the sacrifice is something in which women, menstruating and birth-giving women in particular, do not participate, indeed in which by definition, they cannot participate. The death of Christ celebrated in the Eucharist is therefore remembered as an occasion of exclusion of women at one of the most crucial moments in the history of salvation and yet his sacrificial death makes no theological or ecclesiological sense if it is not seen in the line of the other major events in the history of salvation: the incarnation, Christ born of Mary, as a particular sexual human being through the body of a woman; Easter, the resurrection of Christ, first announced to and proclaimed by women (a reality which those churches of the word who ban women from the pulpit prefer not to be reminded of) and Pentecost, the Spirit of God poured on both men and women to proclaim the gospel and be men and women of God. This is the foundation of the church that celebrates the Eucharist. And another perspective is important here: the sacrifice of Christ, if one chooses to use this metaphor, does not stand without the other sacrifices that were part of it: the sacrifice of Mary, his mother, letting go of her child, not mentioned in this most important celebration of the life of the church.

Along with the sacrificial imagery goes that of the 'great high priest' as Christ, the ultimate mediator of the sacrifice of praise. Again, this is a metaphor of exclusion, describing a reality which, despite the ordination of women, is not accessible to women. What difference does it make to our concept of priesthood and its ecclesiological and liturgical consequences if it is a woman who is celebrating the Eucharist with the whole body of Christ, both men and women who are church? Does priesthood become a metaphor of mere inclusion, of a woman doing a man's job? Or is it a transformed image or one that needs to be replaced by another that takes into account women's lives and bodies as well as the reality of women being excluded from both priesthood and sacrifice?

In 2000, the Church of England published *Common Worship*, its new authorized service book. The existing four eucharistic prayers were replaced by a set of six representing a wider variety of authorized worship in order to prevent people who feel not represented within what is available to 'do their own thing'. David Stancliffe, head of the liturgical commission, argued: 'A framework of order is needed to contain the theological and ecclesiological dangers of diversity' (Stancliffe 1998: 13). Stancliffe continues that 'enough variety in prayer and structure is needed to enable the diversity of cultural communities we serve to pray with integrity and understanding'. The Liturgical Commission is therefore aiming for a variety of structures with common features to reflect what the Church of England is: a very diverse body of believers. Reflecting on the revisions and proposed revisions as well as on the conspicuous absence of women and their presence, I want to ask what the aims for women in liturgical revision are and can be. The fact that Eucharistic Prayer A, a combination of prayers one and two in the *Alternative Service Book*, replaces 'born as man' with 'born of a woman' (which, apart from anything else, is bad poetry, and appears as a token gesture if one realizes that all of the prayers representing a wide variety of traditions still rely on exclusively masculine imagery for God) shows that recommendations for inclusive language, such as replacing the 'sins of all men' with 'the sins of the whole world', to take another example, are by no means replacing exclusive imagery at the most central points.

An interesting example is Eucharistic Prayer D which is recommended for use with children. The response throughout this Eucharistic Prayer, prompted by 'This is our story', is 'This is our song. Hosannah in the highest.' This phrase, taken from a well-known hymn, poses an interesting question for women: if the life of the church is really the telling of Christ's story through the stories of women, men and children and the Eucharist is the most central enactment of this reality, I want to ask if this is really what is happening in the revision of authorized worship in the Church of England. What is at stake for women is, however, not to be token representatives within a variety that includes Catholics, Evangelicals, the Orthodox, the *Alternative Service Book* or even the *Book of Common Prayer*, but rather to respond critically and constructively from their perspective of being church to the liturgical revisions placed before them. The answer cannot be 'gender neutral' rites as if such a thing existed. If we celebrate the Eucharist as women, men and children, our eucharistic rites need to take into account and make explicit the presence and perspective of women being church.

These reflections on the two 'primary' sacraments of baptism and communion, show that feminist ecclesiology is indeed seeking for something new, for different ways of appropriating and rereading the vital concept of sacramental celebration. In her book *Extravagant Affections*, Susan Ross discusses sacramental theology in dialogue with women's experiences on the margins of traditional churches and new liturgical communities (Ross 1998). Ross concludes that what is required by these women is not so much a mere expansion of the traditional canon of sacraments to include women's experiences, but a redefinition of the meaning of sacramentality as such which rings true with their own experiences of embodiment. Susan Roll describes this process as follows:

> Groups of women who come together as subjects to do liturgy for themselves often do not find their own persons, their female bodies, or concrete realities of their daily lives reflected in the defined sacraments, and consequently seek a more authentic yet often diffuse sense of sacramentality as the living presence of God in a multitude of other mediators... Not merely 'complementary' to existing sacramental rites, new women's celebrations experiment with new ways not only to symbolize but to embody the living God, as well as to articulate a vital relationship between liturgy and the making of social justice (Roll 2000: 316).

This new sacramentality manifests itself in new understandings of what it means for the church to be holy. Holiness, according to Mary Grey, is a dynamic reality, which can be found among others in three different locations:

1. the re-discovery of creation spirituality
2. 'in fidelity to the stance of resistance to injustice from the margins'
3. in the recovery of understanding holiness as 'wholeness', 'where the sacredness of relating to God and to each other in the goodness of bodily and sexual feeling is celebrated in an attempt to recover from the over-spiritualized approach of the centuries' (Grey 1997a: 29).

This resistance to domination cannot be restricted to the human sector of creation but involves the whole of creation. The church can no longer claim to be the 'new creation' which supersedes the first and now fallen creation. A feminist sacramental church which makes no distinction between the sacred and the secular has to be an ecological church which takes responsibility for the preservation of creation and the sharing of limited resources. If the starting point for sacramentality is God's revelation in the material, this includes the whole material world and thereby affirms the sacredness of the whole universe. Being church takes place in the world which is the body of God and the temple of human worship of the incarnate divine. The church's struggle for justice has to include the struggle against environmental degradation (Grey 1997b: 71). A sacramental ecclesiology which affirms the human and particularly the female body needs to involve the struggle for environments in which these bodies can flourish, not only on spiritual terms, but starting from the most basic human needs such as clean water, sufficient food supplies and appropriate medical care.

A feminist sacramental ecclesiology cannot remain confined to the limitations of the male-defined canon of sacraments, but ultimately regards being church and all its manifestations as sacramental. This entails moving beyond the separation of word and sacrament as constituting the church in order to regard the sharing of the word of God spoken in the words of women as sacramental. A sacramental ecclesiology seeks to reclaim women's bodies. This also includes reclaiming women's voices. In their experience of church, women have often been reduced to merely being submissive listeners of the word of God preached by men. An embodied sacramental understanding of women's being church, however, discovers sacramental reality also where women are empowered to speak, to tell their own stories of suffering and liberation, where they begin 'to hear each other into speech'.

This reclaiming of the sacramentality of the word, of God's story being told in the stories of women, overcomes centuries of women being silenced purely on the grounds of their being female. It reflects patriarchal selective hearing that St Paul's admonition for women to be silent in church in order to maintain decency and order (which may have been a later conjecture anyway) is quoted more frequently than his assertion of baptismal equality and alleviation of boundaries between the sexes. This shows a fundamental distortion of significance which regards a secondary and contingent instruction regarding church order in a particular community as more important than the message of the gospel itself. This is, for example, reflected in Origen's strict objection to women's speaking in church:

> ...it is improper for a woman to speak in the assembly no matter what she says, even if she says admirable things, or even saintly things, that is of little consequence, since they come from the mouth of a woman (Origen in Malone 2000: 130).

Origen reflects the sentiment of his own time, the culture of third century Hellenism and Judaism, in which women's places were clearly defined as being within the patriarchal family. Feminist ecclesiology is consciously contextual and therefore has to recognize the limitations of such instructions even if they are based on elements of Scripture.

Women's assertion to be church and to always have been church is a sacramental reclaiming of the Christian story as the story of women, the struggle to write women into the Christian narrative, as performers of divine embodiment and speech. This begins with claiming women's presence at the key stages of the gospel narrative, such as recognizing women as the main witnesses of the crucifixion and resurrection, the foundational events of Christian history and the very existence of the church. In doing that, the story of Christ's life and death, the story of incarnation, crucifixion and resurrection, is told and embodied in women's own stories of birth, transformation and death. Women 'hear each other into speech', they name themselves in relation to God and each other. In such hearing, the word itself, the word of God spoken in the words of women, becomes sacramental. Nelle Morton describes this process of speaking and hearing among women:

> A new kind of seeing and hearing was beginning to be experienced by one group of women after the other. Once they recognized in themselves a common oppression, they could hear from one another that which many, more astute and intellectual than they, could not hear. Experiencing grace in this manner has become one of the most liberating forces in the lives of women. It is important that the data that these women shared was out of their living, historical experience. Yet, the new words and the new way old words came to expression, while in the context of history, were not evoked by history. Neither oppression nor suffering shaped their speech. Women came to new speech simply because they were being heard. Hearing became an act of receiving the women as well as the words (Morton 1985: 17).

She describes how being heard and listened, hearing and listening to each other enabled and formed a covenant of liberation between women which, if Morton had been writing in a Christian paradigm, could be described as being church with each other:

> Tasting a liberation they had never known before began to appropriate a new kind of courage to explore the future with no human history to inform and a new ability to articulate that which has never before come to speech. They began to know themselves as persons of worth who would pick up their own lives and be responsible for them. They covenanted together that never again would they allow themselves to become isolated from each other (Morton 1985: 18).

In telling their own stories, women confess, they proclaim the presence of the living God in their shared lives, they speak out against the sinful structures of the patriarchal church and society and name each other as those who are the church against which the gates of patriarchy will not prevail. Such a sacramental understanding of women's words identifies Women-Church not as a closed narrow institution by which grace and salvation are dispensed, but as an open space in which women, men and children are able to celebrate their own and each other's being in the image of God.

# Chapter Seven

# Beyond 'In' or 'Out':
# Reframing the Ecclesiological Debate

In 1893, the leader of the National Women's Suffrage Association, Matilda Joslyn Gage, described the Christian Church as the 'prime source of oppression for women'. In order to be liberated, she wrote, women must throw off both Christianity and all patriarchal legal codes shaped by Christianity. Gage was not and is not alone in her identification of the Christian Church as oppressive for women and certainly not in her claim to leave the church behind. And yet this is not what this book has been about. I have already pointed out that doing feminist ecclesiology essentially means moving beyond the choice of either leaving or staying, but means a conscious choice to claim and reclaim being church for women and as women. It is the shared embodiment of their (Christian) faith as communities of subversive sacramentality and constructive resistance.

Feminist ecclesiological reflection is a discourse which takes place on a variety of different planes: it involves the reclaiming and rereading of traditional structures and concepts as well as the creative and constructive development of new communities and their practices of faith and spirituality. Its starting point is the lived and embodied faith, worship and action of those who participate in faith communities old and new, but it also reflects critically on those theological concepts which shaped such discourses. Its aim is transformation of the church as a site of meaning into a body of those whose shared lives embody and proclaim the values of the reign of God and in doing that participate and share in the life of the Triune God. Such activity is essentially subversive. It involves a claiming and reclaiming of the power centres of the church and a reshaping of such discourses of power according to a feminist reconsideration of power as well as a redefinition of what makes the church and how its subversive activity of being the body of Christ can take place.

Catherine Mowry LaCugna, in her work on the divine Trinity, describes ecclesial life as follows:

> Ecclesial life is a way of living in anticipation of the coming reign of God. The church makes a claim that civil governments do not: that it is the People of God, Body of Christ, and Temple of the Holy Spirit. The life of the church is to be animated by the life of God; the church is to embody in the world the presence of the risen Christ, showing by its preaching and by its own form of life that sin and death have been overcome by Jesus Christ. The church also claims to embody in its corporate life the presence, fruits, and work of the Holy Spirit, to be a visible sign of God's reign, of the divine-human communion, and the communion of all creatures with one another. In sum, the church claims to live the form of life appropriate to God's economy, to point to the reign of God within the *oikumen*, the whole inhabited earth (LaCugna 1991: 401).

According to LaCugna, the life of the church together with 'sacramental life, ethical life, and sexual life will be seen clearly as forms of Trinitarian life: living God's life with one another' (LaCugna 1991: 411).

While groups like the Women-Church movement worked with the assumption of an essentially modern context, and a liberal, voluntarist and pragmatist agenda, feminist ecclesiology at the beginning of the third millennium of the Christian discourse needs to embrace its postmodern context while always being prepared to subvert it at the same time. Feminist ecclesiological discourse takes place on the boundary: it embraces existing institutional structures as well as the discourses of faith of those who reject those structures for a variety of reasons and identify the locations of their spirituality elsewhere. This therefore means a reconsideration of what is meant by 'church' in feminist ecclesiological reflections. Where do women's discourses of spirituality take place and in what way are they subversive of existing structures and narratives? And how do these multiple locations and transformed and transforming discourses impact on a reframing of ecclesiology?

Many women no longer found the church a meaningful location for their discourses of faith and spirituality and as a response left the established churches in large numbers. Mary Daly's symbolic 'exodus' out of Harvard Memorial Church symbolizes that the churches' identification with patriarchy provoked women's disaffection with the church. Daly understands the church and Christianity, indeed all organized religion, as the prime means of patriarchy to generate and enforce the subordination of women. In *Beyond God the Father*, Daly describes 'sisterhood' as 'cosmic antichurch', the ultimate denial of patriarchal religion which is in fact all religion (Daly 1973: 132). According to Daly, religion in all its forms and aspects, and religious institutions such as churches in particular, are intrinsically connected with patriarchy and cannot be understood as anything but its most powerful means of self-justification. Therefore women must leave behind all religious institutions and religion itself, and enter the cosmic covenant of sisterhood. Daly sees this leaving behind as not only necessary, but as essentially positive: 'It is the bringing forth into the world of New Being, which by its very coming annihilates the credibility of myths contrived to support the structures of alienation' (Daly 1973: 139). The only way women can be saved from patriarchy is by entering into the radically new Being of sisterhood which replaces the silence, the non-being, imposed on women by patriarchal religion:

> The New Being of Antichurch is a rising up of Mother and Daughter together, beyond the Madonna's image and beyond the ambivalent Warrior Maiden's image. The togetherness comes from nonimmersion [*sic*] in either role and it comes from our desperation which has made us remember and look forward to the Golden Age (Daly 1973: 150).

Daly denies the church all empowering potential for women, and views the church mainly as an institution, the primary purpose of which is to destroy women and to jeopardize women's liberation. This essentially denies centuries of women's history within the church and attempts to replace women's existing traditions within the church with an ideal of women's sisterhood that bears the same potential to be transformed into either destructive anarchy or a restrictive institution like the patriarchal church. Daly's concept of 'sisterhood' remains essentially disembodied and obsessed with the destructive forces of patriarchy which attack women's bodies, so that it overlooks the transformative presence of women's bodies embodying the body of Christ. Therefore her project of sisterhood as the post-patriarchal anti-church cannot be of use to the feminist transformation of ecclesiology, as it essentially remains at the stage of deconstruction without taking account of the constructive power already present in women's being church. Daly's rejection of religion as a potentially meaningful space for women essentially blocks all historical enquiry as it does not recognize women's history of struggling against patriarchal structures and their attempts to create their own discourses of faith within a patriarchal church as meaningful. Such an approach therefore cannot be of use to the development of feminist ecclesiology, as feminist ecclesiology seeks to affirm what Daly denies: women's being church within a framework of Christianity which is not necessarily confined to man-made institutional boundaries, but at the same time recognizes these institutions as spaces where meaningful discourses of faith have taken place for women throughout history. The aim of feminist ecclesiology therefore cannot be to make a blanket judgment about the history of the Christian Church as being infested with patriarchy in order to focus on a post-patriarchal future. This would mean to deny one of the fundamental tenets of Christianity itself: Christianity is a historical religion based on the reality of the incarnation having taken place within the confinement of time and space. Feminist church history is therefore concerned with history and the way the history of the church is written. Patriarchy as a dominant force both in history itself and in what is recorded as relevant is as much a reality as women's discourses of faith which have taken place within it and often in spite of it.

The North American Women-Church movement is an attempt of women to declare their independence from existing institutional churches and to declare their own discourses of being church loosely within the framework of Christianity. The core of the Women-Church movement was the founding of a loose network of women's organizations concerned with spirituality and justice, the Women-Church Convergence. The Women-Church movement can in part be seen as a response to the disappointment with renewal movements within the church, such as the Second Vatican Council. At the heart of the Women-Church movement are small liturgical base communities in which women meet to celebrate feminist rituals and discuss their own reflections on being church. The traditional, patriarchal church can no longer claim to be the sole representation of church. Women-Church does not understand itself as a new authoritative institution, but rather as a support network for its various members in their shared commitment to spirituality, sexuality and justice as factors of what it means to be church. They are committed to women being full agents in the life of the church whose contribution to ministry, justice work and sacramental life is essential for the lives of different churches. Primary goals of the work of Women-Church are the equal distribution of resources, the elimination of racism, sexism and heterosexism and the eradication of violence. Liturgy and ritual are part of the life of Women-Church, but are far from being the only form of activity. The involvement of both liturgical groups and organizations working for the establishment of social justice shows that Women-Church does not understand itself as a religious movement which can be separated from political activity, but that being church, life as church, is always first and foremost political praxis. Women-Church is not the replacement of one set of potentially oppressive structures with another but the weaving of connections between those who share their praxis of faith as a commitment to justice for all.

Movements such as Women-Church challenge feminist church historians to see the egalitarian vision of Christian origins as the key paradigm which needs to be dis-covered as existent throughout the history of Christianity in order to be re-covered so that it may in turn transform the Church. This means to acknowledge that the existing institutional churches are not the only framework within which women's discourses of faith and equality have taken place and to include other frameworks of women's discourses of faith into what feminist theologians study.

Feminist ecclesiology seeks to identify, research, record and interpret women's discourses of Christian faith. These are discourses of telling the story of God through their own stories, discourses of embodiment and performance of creation, incarnation and salvation. Women challenge the churches' understandings of themselves by claiming their embodiment of God's story as part of what it means to be church. These are discourses of authority, discourses of authorship, of ecclesiological *écriture feminine* which challenge women's church history as a discipline and as an interdisciplinary discourse to rethink its subject matter and not to allow that subject matter to be restricted by man-made boundaries and institutions.

As we have seen throughout this book, women's discourses of spirituality take place on a variety of different levels and in a variety of different locations. One of the aspects shared by all of them, though, is that for most women these discourses do involve a corporate and communal and therefore a public and political element. This is what feminist ecclesiology essentially seeks to discuss in terms of theological discourse and language. This corporate element is also one of the key aspects of the subversive nature of feminist ecclesiology as corporate identity is not a value proclaimed in postmodern, post-Thatcher Britain at large. Grace Davie describes the spiritual discourses of many members of contemporary British society as 'believing not belonging' (Davie 1994). Feminist ecclesiology, however, speaks about providing open spaces in which women's diverse embodied discourses of spirituality, in dialogue with the Christian tradition, are valued and shared as part of that tradition and yet also as a subversion of the institutions and boundaries which that very tradition has created for women.

Feminist ecclesiology at the beginning of the third millennium is essentially a political discourse. Its starting point is not the church as an institution, but the world in which women (and men) who are church live. It needs to take seriously and yet subvert the main characteristics of this world, those of increasing fragmentation and yet also globalization, which together leave many in a crisis of identity and belonging. Traditional discourses of being the Christian Church have made universalist claims about the church being a spiritual and physical body that transcends all boundaries of nationality and historical development. At the same time, ecclesiology is always contextual and takes place within the confinements of the historical realities of time, space and political ordering of society. Feminist ecclesiology at the beginning of the third millennium needs to inquire into the effects that developments of fragmentation, such as the end of the socio-political ordering of the Cold War in Eastern Europe, have for women in their particular contexts and what impact these developments have on their being church. While an awareness and taking account of the fragmented lives of women in today's world is obviously part of the agenda of feminist discourses of being church, the actual task and identity of the church needs to go beyond that. Being church, offering corporate identity that acknowledges and yet transcends the various aspects of belonging in women's lives, means to provide a new focus, an attempt to 'gather the fragments', as Mary Grey puts it (Grey 1997a: 40). Mary Grey argues that traditional models of church provide little to no inspiration for the development of new ways of being church in subversion of a fragmented world.

Following Mark Cline Taylor, Mary Grey identifies three areas in which being church responds to the claims made by postmodernity:

1.   a sense of tradition (or, as Grey calls it, traditioning)
2.   a celebration of plurality; and
3.   resistance to domination (Grey 1997a: 37).

These represent essential forms of subversion as they are embodied by feminist discourses of ecclesiology and being church. Feminist ecclesiology takes place in constant dialogue with the Christian tradition and challenges the powers which identify what is regarded as relevant tradition and what is not. This involves the discovery of hidden traditions as well as the creative and constructive development of new traditions and new readings of traditional discourses of being church.

Plurality, the affirmation of diversity, as described perhaps in using the kitchen-table metaphor as an image for what it means to be church, is another important characteristic of feminist ways of being church. This is rooted in belief in the incarnation as God Godself becoming one particular human being, which is at the heart of the Christian faith. In celebrating human particularity and diversity for themselves and with others, women participate in the church as the continuation of the incarnation. Such plurality, which is different from pluralism as a characteristic of postmodernity, identifies church as a platform for dialogue and mutual affirmation as well as constructive conflict and as such subverts centralistic structures of ecclesial government.

I have already identified ecclesiology as a public discourse which challenges all structures of injustice and socio-economic exploitation. Resistance against domination and the prophetic development of structures and discourses of equality and justice is a key characteristic of being church that must permeate all dimensions of ecclesial life. Grey describes the current situation of the existing church as a dark night which needs to be challenged, reformed and essentially transformed. She proposes to work towards a feminist theology of contemplation as 'the means to the recovery of community, and in order to find a way of staying with the struggle and re-sourcing it in a way that frees new energy for gathering and re-shaping the cultural fragments' (Grey 1997b: 6). Grey sees prophecy and mysticism as vital resources for the rebuilding of the church in an age of crisis. In these two final chapters of constructive proposals of how a feminist ecclesiology could work, I would like to build on Grey's work amongst others and take it further into dialogue with both the existing ecclesiological traditions and feminist ecclesiology in particular. I have already mentioned that feminist ecclesiology has to work on a variety of different levels. It has to reclaim the power centres of traditional churches, such as the preaching of the word, the celebration of the sacraments and any other form of worship, understandings of ministry, both lay and ordained, the church's understanding of mission and many other aspects of the praxis and the theological self-reflection of the church. Yet at the same time, feminist ecclesiology proposes a refocusing of the ecclesiological debate; in other words, it seeks to develop new ways of thinking about what actually makes the church the church in this present context and how the church, whatever form it takes, can be the church at this moment in time, responding to this particular cluster of questions. The question is therefore: what are the resources on which the church can draw in order to be a place in which meaningful discourses of women's and men's spirituality and social action can take place that are inspired by the Christian message? Mary Grey proposes prophecy and mysticism, which I will explore further; I would like to add a third: poetics. Yet, the list is by no means closed: all three stand for a wide range of means/resources of resistance and subversion which can embody the life of the Triune God in today's world.

Mary Grey argues that mystical spirituality is not a private search for deeper communion with the divine, but rather always rooted in the struggle of a particular community and a response to the questions raised by that struggle:

> ...what seems particularly to characterize the mystics is the desire to communicate God's revelation, always within the humble consciousness that language is a poor vehicle. So the hunger for a mystical and contemplative faith is not the *private* search for comfort in the experience of lostness [*sic*] and current confusion; it springs from the existential angst of our time, from the struggle against despair and the determination to keep hope alive (Grey 1997b: 10).

Prophecy, for Grey, is likewise rooted in the community; in fact, communities themselves in their counter-cultural living, rather than merely outstanding individuals within them, are meant to be prophetic, to live in a prophetic way. Prophecy always has a dimension of uncomfortable truth-telling. Prophets have throughout the history of the Hebrew and Christian traditions been voices of disruption. Women's being church takes place in a framework of fundamental ambiguity. A further expression of this ambiguity is the tension between making a spiritual home for themselves, as women do in founding their own liturgical communities, and singing God's song in a strange land. The stranger is the one who is able to ask uncomfortable questions and by doing so reminds the community/church of the very purpose of its own being: to be a community of justice, an anticipation of God's reign on earth, a forth-telling of God's story of creation and incarnation. Women-Church is a hermeneutical space, a reading community. Its reading is, however, not confined to the texts prescribed by a particular tradition, but it includes a critical and constructive reading of all experiences, of the whole of creation in the light of the values of the reign, the kin-dom of the Triune God's being-in-relation.

Women who choose to stay within existing denominational or ecclesial structures seek to 'preach a liberating *ekklesia* in the midst of ecclesiastical rigidity' (Winter *et al*. 1994: 63). Women who are involved in groups such as the Catholic Women's Network or Catholic Women's Ordination have chosen to move beyond the choice of opting in or opting out, but claim their being church within an existing tradition which still holds meaning for them:

> ...it's not their church, it's not Rome's church, it's *our* church. We don't have to fight for a place in the church, because lay women and lay men *are* the church, the body of Christ. It is my conviction that this is so, manifest in my own life in a deep love for the sacramental tradition and ritual of the Roman Catholic Church that keeps me at home here (Winter *et al*. 1994: 65).

One group of women who have been involved in creating Women-Church as a space of liberation for the whole church are Roman Catholic sisters, often educated as well or better than the priests who were called into their communities to say Mass and hear their confessions. Roman Catholic sisters in the USA have put together a list of goals they want to have reached by the year 2010:

> Converted by the example of Jesus and the values of the gospel, we would serve a prophetic role in church and society by critiquing values and structures and calling for systemic change.

> Converted by the marginalized, we would invest resources in advocacy for structural change on behalf of the poor and oppressed and work to change the locus of power from models of domination to collaborative models of power-sharing and decision-making.

> Understanding ourselves as church, we would assume our priestly role of shared
> leadership in the life and worship of the local church; and we would see
> ourselves as centers of the experience of God and of a spirituality of wholeness,
> global connectedness, and reverence for the earth (Winter *et al.* 1994: 110).

Feminist ecclesiology seeks to transform the existing churches as well as create new structures. These are based on the strong desire among women to make the church a place where justice is done and right relationships can be formed in a framework of interconnectedness and participation:

> The just church would be participatory and would foster relationships, be a place
> to express doubt and struggle, a place to test beliefs, a place to deal with prob-
> lems, where there is acknowledgement of conflicts and the will to work things
> out, where there is openness to multiple interpretations of the spiritual life,
> where there is commitment on the part of all to go out and help God to trans-
> form the world. It would be a microcosm of the just world, not only counter-
> cultural but transcultural. The just church would be a global church, an
> international democratic institution and it would make a difference. It would use
> its power for good (Winter *et al.* 1994: 192).

Being church and creating/incarnating church in the world is a poetic process. It involves women's search for a new language of faith and of justice, a language beyond rigidity. The writing of poetry, the creation of art or the writing and performance of music has often been a dangerous and subversive practice which at the same time is an expression of the continuity and indestructibility of life amidst turmoil and death. Poetics is a counter-discourse that disrupts discourses of suffering and oppression and transcends them by re-membering beauty and ultimately the divine. It is a manifestation of divine creativity and incarnationality. It is a form of reconnecting with the divine and with women's selves as well as with each other. Poetry and art have often been confined and restricted throughout the Christian tradition by limiting their use to the context of institutionalized worship. Women have often been excluded from being recognized as creators and performers of such liturgical music or poetry, for example by not permitting mixed choirs to sing from the sanctuary. Poetics as a resource for the church at the beginning of the third millennium stands for all aspects of creative activity, be they the writing of poetry, the performing arts, art and creativity in the development of new communities and healthy human relations. In being involved in constructive creativity, women participate in the work of God Godself who is creator and redeemer of the whole of creation. This creativity is essentially shared creativity as it seeks the expression of an individual or a group of individuals for the good of the whole of creation. It is the overcoming of the subject-object divide prevalent in consumerist society, as the creator, the created and those who share in the creation become one in the celebration of divine, human and earth community.

By being church, women claim their own lives as the presence of the divine in the world. Being church is no longer restricted to patriarchal power centres such as institutions and particular ministries, but church takes place where women and men become aware of their living as church. Their being church breaks the binary, overcomes the dualistic division between the material and the sacred, as women and men discover their own lives in relation and community as sacred presence and sacred community:

> The distancing of sacred reality and revelation from the lived context of communities of faith is a strange phenomenon in a religious tradition founded on belief in incarnation. If Christianity has anything of value to offer to a world in danger of total ecological and/or nuclear destruction, it is in its affirmation of sacred presence in and among physical realities, including but not limited to all human persons. This affirmation does not deny the *transcendence* of the divine, when transcendence is understood in its root sense of 'crossing over'. If incarnation implies the 'crossing over' of the boundaries between human and divine, then these two facets of Christian belief are integral to one another... Creative resistance to dominating structures requires insistence upon the possibility of revelation through a multitude of diverse expressions by incarnate beings (Wetherilt 1994: 16; italics original).

What makes such ecclesiological discourse, such claiming and reclaiming women's lives as church Christian? Within the Women-Church convergence, by no means all of its member communities claim allegiance to the Christian tradition. In addition, I have emphasized the profound openness of feminist ecclesiology to a diversity of traditions and discourses of faith which transcends the boundaries of man-made institutional frameworks. Nevertheless, the use of the word 'church' does imply a connection to the Christian tradition that I would not want to surrender as it has been meaningful and life-giving for women throughout the ages. For some women, this connection is found in identification and fascination with the person of Jesus as he is presented in the synoptic gospels, while they often acknowledge difficulties with the narrow christological focus of ecclesiology in, for example, the nuptial metaphor, which describes the church as the bride of Christ. It is therefore important to transcend this christological focus and to expand my ecclesiology by seeing Jesus Christ, if he is to be a meaningful reference point for our discourses of faith, organized or individual, regular or occasional, as part of the wider Trinitarian being of God. Some feminist theologians seek to rediscover the third person of the divine Trinity, the Holy Spirit, as a means of overcoming the (at times) unhealthy christological focus of ecclesiology. This is certainly an important development as it expresses the freedom and the presence of the divine throughout creation and not confined to particular historical institutions. On the other hand, however, I would argue that no wholistic (*sic*) and wholesome feminist ecclesiology can be contented with focusing on just one person of the divine Trinity. Divine being in relation is essentially the being in communion of all three persons, and women seeking to reclaim their presence in communion with the divine are challenged to reclaim the whole of God, the whole of the church and the whole of creation.

A further reference point with the Christian tradition and a starting point for its reclaiming as church is a possible rereading of the idea of the church as one, holy, catholic and apostolic. In the Creed, the framework of faith acknowledged by a variety of Christian Churches through the ages, these marks of the church are acknowledged. Yet what do they mean for a new feminist reconsideration of ecclesiology?

The unity of the church is often expressed as a characteristic desirable above all. Yet in many women's experience, it is also used as an excuse to hear the voices of women and acknowledge women's gifts and vocations in the church, for example, in the debate about the ordination of women in the Church of England where some voices believe that the Church of England as a local church does not have the right to make a unilateral decision to ordain women as this would diminish any chances for a reunion with the Roman Catholic and the Orthodox Churches. Is this the unity which is meant or is desirable in the context of Women-Church? Or are we talking about a different form of unity, a unity in diversity which is found in God's own being in relation, a unity which celebrates the diverse expression within the Christian tradition and the diverse stories and lives which perform and manifest the story of God with the church and the whole of creation? It is not a unity which seeks to avoid conflict and ambiguity at all costs, but is able to live within the ambiguity of God's reign as manifest on earth, in the struggle for justice and right relations for all.

The idea of the church's holiness has also been used to oppress women in the church throughout its history. Women were, and still are, on the grounds of their supposed ritual impurity, banned from sacred ministries and from entry into the sanctuary. Holy men, clerical or other, are those who stay away from women as sources of defilement, and holy women are those who manage to deny or reject their female sexuality. Yet, we have to ask: whose holiness is the holiness of the church? Is it that of a community which withdraws from the world in order to avoid sin, and as a result creates its own sinful patriarchal oppressive structures in which women are forced to submit to men by default? Is it the holiness of a select and separate community which avoids its own mission to be present in the world, to be the leaven in the lump of the world, to challenge its sinful structures of injustice by living justly with each other and the whole of creation? Or is it the holiness of God creative and incarnate who became human and manifests God's own being in humanity and in the church in the world? God's holiness and that of the church manifests itself in living as God lives in the world, in a commitment to those to whom God is committed, the poor and oppressed and the whole suffering creation. It is a holiness that is not afraid of defilement, but one which recognizes its own participation in sinful structures of patriarchy and oppression and yet seeks to live in communities of justice and solidarity with all.

The church is also traditionally described as catholic. Catholicity means universality, the church is the same wherever, whenever and by whomever it exists and manifests itself. It transcends the boundaries of this world and the next by its existence in past, present and future. It knows no geographical, racial or sexual boundaries and yet it is deeply rooted in the particular cultures in which it takes place. Black majority churches, for example, have emphasized the importance of their particular cultural history as a vital resource for their being church. Yet women's experience of the church has often been that of boundaries and limitations, of being the Other rather than being fully affirmed as part of the body of Christ. Catholicity is often understood as an eschatological reality which is used to verify authority rather than affirm those who are church. From a feminist point of view, catholicity means openness, the affirmation of all those who wish to be part of the body that is the church. The breaking of boundaries of race, sex or class is not an eschatological reality, something that will come true in the next world, but something which has to be seen in this world for the church to be the church. By claiming their own being church, women remind the church of its own catholicity, of the universality of its vocation.

The idea of apostolicity and the apostolic succession has also been used as a means of rejecting women and identifying them as not fully part of the body of Christ. The apostolic succession of ministries is often falsely understood as a chain of hands being laid on heads in the context of ordination. Extreme groups refuse to recognize not only the apostolicity of the ministries of women ordained, but also the ministry of those who 'defiled' their hands by ordaining women and thereby stepping outside the line of the church catholic and apostolic. The idea of the church apostolic is tainted with a 'theology of taint' which renders women's being church invalid by reducing the authority and the whole existence of the church to a male-defined and patriarchal system of administration. Such an ecclesiology is not authentic to women. Can the apostolicity of the church be reclaimed? First of all, we have to ask: whose apostolicity is it? The Creed speaks of the church apostolic rather than the apostolic succession. I therefore want to assert that true apostolicity is always the apostolicity of the whole church, not that of a particular group of its ministers. It is the life of the church as the continuation of the vision of the earliest Christian communities which feminist theologians such as Elisabeth Schüssler Fiorenza and others have reconstructed as one of equality and justice for all, a vision in which women's ministries and lives were affirmed and celebrated. Fiorenza has shown in her work that this vision, despite the increasing patriarchalization of the church in its Graeco-Roman context, has never entirely died out, but has continued to be created and recreated in a variety of different movements that have affirmed women's equality and ministry.

In reframing the ecclesiological debate, feminist theologians affirm the church as one, holy, catholic and apostolic, as the church which celebrates diversity, which is committed to a vision of justice and equality which is God's vision, a church which is open to all and the whole of creation, and a church which seeks to embody the vision of the earliest Christian communities and to re-enact it in a multiplicity of different contexts.

Being church is not the creation or recreation of an institution or even a charismatic community, but the description of a dynamic process of transformation and change. Feminist ecclesiology can therefore not be the description of such an institution, the search for new metaphors or even the reconstruction of particular structures. Some feminist theologians in their search for new ways of speaking about God have moved from speaking of God as a person to speaking about God as a verb, such as 'godding', in order to express the dynamic reality of God's being in relation. I propose a similar shift in a feminist understanding of church. As I have shown in this book, a feminist understanding of church needs to take into account those who are church and be authentic to them rather than see the church as an entity which is somehow separate from them. Feminist theology can therefore not talk about the church as such, or women and the church, but has as its subject nothing other than women's being church. Being church is a dynamic, active process: a crossing of man-made boundaries, the creation and transformation of right relationships. Women's being church is movement, transformation, an opening up to others and to the whole of creation. In such dynamic movements, God is embodied here and now. The church of the Word is transformed into the multiple communities who speak in their own voices and hear each other into speech:

> A theological metaphor of a static and unitary Word cannot incorporate the voices of God that echo in the lives of diverse beings and the earth on which they live. The written text, and its successor, electronic data storage, will contribute to voicing God in the world to the extent that those who generate such texts understand their voices to be but one expression of revelation. In the midst of the day-to-day lives of multiple communities and individuals, and especially in their relationships with one another, God is voiced through struggle and celebration, self-defense and education, spirited worship and birthing a baby, writing poetry and planting maize. As these many voices of justice—echoes of God—come into increasing dialogue with each other, possibilities are enhanced for the coming of the kin-dom, now and forever (Wetherilt 1994: 149).

One of the inevitable limitations of feminist ecclesiology so far has been its focus on the Western understanding of the church as an institution which has to be reformed or left behind. This, in my opinion, does not go far enough in terms of a reframing of ecclesiology. Doing ecclesiology in a feminist paradigm means transcending the man-made boundaries of the schism between East and West and searching the whole of the Christian tradition for meaningful metaphors and models of thinking of being church. I therefore suggest a closer dialogue with the ecclesiologies of the Christian East. These cannot, of course, be taken as they are, and the reflective feminist reader has to be aware of the patriarchal and androcentric bias in which they were conceived and written. Yet they too are a cluster of traditions in which women have participated and with which they have been and are in dialogue. John Zizioulas, in his book *Being as Communion*, defines church not so much as an institution but as a mode of being, a way of existence (Zizioulas 1985). Through baptism and participation in the Eucharist, human beings become and are what they are meant to be, human beings who participate in the divine communion and therefore in the shared personhood of God. What could a feminist rereading of this concept look like? Women are church and have always been church. In becoming church, women do not become part of another, their being is not defined by another, not even God, but women become authentic to themselves and as such can be in relation to others and to the whole of creation. Being church means becoming aware of and acknowledging the sacramental reality of the interconnected web of life which is creation and communion. Being church does not mean becoming someone else, acting in a way which is imposed by someone else, but embodying God within us as women. It means taking authority, authorship in doing justice, in caring for each other and for the whole of creation, in hearing each other's stories and telling our own and in doing that telling the story of God. Ecclesiology in the traditional frameworks of theology has had its place between theological anthropology and eschatology, between theological reflection on what it means to be human in the constructive tension between being in the image of God and living in structures of sin and sinfulness and the theological reflection on the 'last things', the world in the light of God's creativity and justice. Being church takes place in thinking who we are in relation to others and to the whole of creation and in thinking how we can create structures of God's justice and right relation not only in the next world but already in this one. This cannot be done in isolation but only as part of a community of shared responsibility, creativity and celebration. Luce Irigaray argues that women should not merely seek representation in human institutions but their place in God's own being (Irigaray 1997). In the context of doing feminist ecclesiology this is realized: being church is women's claim to the authority of being the actualization of God's being as communion in this world and with this world.

# Chapter Eight

# Communities that Embody the Story of God: Towards a Feminist Narrative Ecclesiology

So, what is the church and who is it? As I have shown in this book, feminist ecclesiology ultimately seeks to disrupt the binary frameworks in which traditional reflections on the church have sought to operate. We cannot simply discard the institutional church and opt for the church as a dynamic and charismatic community. We cannot think about women's discourses of faith by categorizing them as either inside or outside the church. Feminist ecclesiology combines analysis of and reflection on the existing structures with a prophetic critique and challenge. Feminist ecclesiology is essentially about radical openness to the continuing story of the divine with this world and to the many stories, told and untold, of women of faith. The church needs to be rethought and reconstructed as a place where women can hear each other into speech. Such a 'hearing into speech' is sacramental and creates the fabric of which the church is made. Without hearing women's stories of faith, of oppression and liberation, the story of God is not told. This telling of stories and hearing into speech takes many different forms. Gavin D'Costa argues:

> If the liturgy does not celebrate both women and men, both in terms of the human and the divine, then the liturgy cannot be the praise of God by the entire church. Neither is it simply a matter of politically correct liturgies... Inclusivism, or equalism, is not what is at stake, but the creation of a new ecclesiological economy of redeeming signs, so that the Marian body of Christ might provide a different story. The story will not sound the same (D'Costa 2000: 199).

The Catholic tradition has always retained a certain amount of awareness of the need to tell the stories of human beings of faith as part of telling the story of God. This is also the story of the church in the notion of the communion of saints as the body of those who witness with their lives and deaths to the story of the gospel and intercede on behalf of those living as church today before

God. While recognizing the hierarchical constraints with which this notion of sainthood and canonization has been burdened, there has been a renewed interest among feminist theologians in recovering and redeeming the communion of saints as a way of acknowledging women as bearers of faith within the Christian Church and as role models and companions for those who are struggling to be church today.

Yet the stories of the saints of the past are only one part of the story that is the church. Telling their stories is an essentially liberating and community-building process for women that enables them to reclaim the authority which the patriarchal church has so long denied them. Feminist ecclesiology has a personal rather than an institutional focus:

> In telling their story women found their voice and the power to speak with authority. Today feminists no longer accept all that the church is saying simply because it has said it. They are evaluating institutional theology and praxis in the light of their own experience and they are finding the institution wanting (Winter *et al.* 1994: 6).

The process of telling their stories highlights that Women-Church needs to be rooted in the actual lives and concerns of women. These are often of a largely practical nature to the point of ensuring physical survival. It is this lack of concern for women's lives and the achievement of political and social justice that women have found in the existing churches and which drives them to the margins and to develop new structures which are more authentic to the realities of their own lives.

Pamela Dickey Young describes the church as

> a diverse collection of communities of eros who find their common identity in the shared memory and presence of Jesus Christ and seek to embody God's transforming grace by fostering flourishing and right relationship for all creation (Young 2000: 4).

Flourishing and right relation are not what comes to mind when the majority of women reflect on their experience of church. What Young proposes is in many ways a vision of what the church ought to be and what it has begun to be in some places already. What I have tried to show in this book is that feminist ecclesiology operates within a creative tension between women's experiences of church as a site of marginalization and oppression and as a site of empowerment due to the shared memory of the life, death and gospel of Jesus Christ. At the heart of feminist ecclesiology is the struggle for justice and the creation of right relationships, relationships of mutual respect and justice. The *ekklesia* of women, men and children exists and has always existed in the search for right relation and flourishing and in the sacramental telling of stories of suffering and empowerment of those who are beginning to find them.

That women, men and children begin to find spaces in which they can flourish and enable each other to flourish and live in relationships of justice, is rooted in the story of the Triune God sharing God's own being with human-kind and in doing so sharing their being. The Triune God became a particular human being so that particular human beings might flourish as the people they are and share their lives with each other as they are sharing in God's life. Such sharing is possible as human beings live in the tension of being fully themselves and transcending the limitations and boundaries of their own lives as they share the lives of others and of God. This is where being church begins to happen.

Being church means living in relationships which are both transcendent and subversive. They transcend the limitations of gender and power structures imposed on human beings by living within sinful kyriarchal structures and thereby enable them to subvert these very structures in order to create right relationships and justice empowered by the vision of God's being in relation. Pamela Dickey Young writes:

> To flourish is to exist as fully as possible, given that we never exist alone, but always as community with the others, human and non-human, with whom we share the planet. Flourishing, then, is about the whole of life, not about some small part of it, and about how all the parts relate to the whole, both of one's individual life and of one's life in world community (Young 2000: 14).

The life of the church is both bounded and open. It is bounded by the shared memory of Jesus Christ, the story which is embodied and told by those who share in it, as well as acknowledging the choice of those who opt not to share it. It is open to others and to the whole of creation as God's being is open and lives by sharing itself with others.

Feminist ecclesiology transcends the patriarchal demand for an either/or, for opting in or opting out, for leaving one institution in order to join or create another. Feminist ecclesiology is essentially a process which combines a variety of different spaces, locations of meaningful spiritual discourses in the lives of women. It takes place on the brink, on the margins of institutions and organizations, in the creation of networks and connections, in affirming meaningful traditions and the hidden history of our fore-sisters and by creating new traditions. Women's being church encompasses the whole of women's lives and is not restricted to the confines of an institution.

So, what are the characteristics which feminist ecclesiology advocates in order to analyse different ecclesial contexts?

1. The question is not: what is the church? but who is the church? The

church is a space in which women can flourish and celebrate their being in the image of the divine. Dorothea McEwan describes this shift from institution to community:

> ...the churches are seen and experienced not as communities for their believers, their point of growth and involvement, the focal points of their love and engagement for and in society, but as oppressive institutions. To practise the gospel message, however, involves commitment of the faithful towards the non-baptized as well as the baptized members of their society. Thus the feminist vision of community involves more than just leading a prayerful life as an individual and servicing one's own church institution in uncritical obedience. It means a transformation from the pursuit of narrow personal piety alone to the pursuit of and engagement in societal concerns, to being in communion with the community, offering fellowship and partnership, equality and wholeness to fragmented, atomized, segmented societies (McEwan 1991: 252).

2.  This means that the focus is not on the church as an institution, but on the church as a community of people whose diversity is endorsed and celebrated. This, however, does not mean an unrealistically idealistic view of community but one that acknowledges both the significance of the continuity with the Christian tradition and the disruptions to their flourishing that women experience, both in their lives and in the lives of the community. This includes a refusal to be restricted by patriarchal confines of being in or out of the church. Women's being church is essentially open to others as well as to the non-human creation.

3.  Feminist ecclesiology proclaims the church as an embodied community which enables sacramental celebration of the story of God embodied in the lives and bodies of women both past and present. Yet embodiment cannot be restricted to women's bodies alone. Our celebration of being church has to include other aspects such as seeking a church which is affirmative and open to the unconventional bodies of those often constructed as outsiders in society, such as people with disabilities. It therefore has to affirm embodiment in all aspects of its life, starting with the construction of the spaces in which church celebrations and meetings take place. It also needs to take into account the different voices of human beings at different stages in their lives, such as children and young people. Children are not merely the church of tomorrow, but they are, as the people they are now, church, and need to be included and heard into speech.

4.  Feminist ecclesiology proclaims the church as the community which through sacramental hearing each other into speech performs the story of God. Women-Church is a community of justice which advocates the flourishing of all human beings and essentially the whole of creation. Serene Jones writes:

> This church…doesn't just attend to the formation of its own. It seeks practices
> that honor the bodies of all people. Health-care reform, adequate state aid for
> children, excellent public child care, livable [sic] workplace regulations—the
> church is an advocate for these in the broader culture as well as in its own midst.
> It has a positive vision of the kind of space human beings need to flourish.
> Recognizing the grace that envelops and defines the integrity of all creation, this
> church contests institutions and practices that fracture and diminish, such as
> economic exploitative structures, hazardous ecological practices, and degrading
> cultural representations (Jones 2000: 173).

The renewed and transformed church which feminist ecclesiology envisages is one which rejects all violence, be it actual, such as sexual harassment or rape, or spiritual such as the Vatican's indictment to discuss the matter of women's ordination.

5. One of the key characteristics of feminist ecclesiology is that it is essentially an open ecclesiology. The church is not a closed community in which some are in and others are out, but it is a round-table community where everyone is welcome. Hospitality and justice are to be added as marks to unity, catholicity, holiness and apostolicity. The members of the community are open to each other and celebrate their diversity. The community is open to other traditions, even other faiths. The Women-Church movement, for example, includes groups and individual members which incorporate elements of goddess spirituality into their discourses of faith. The church, envisioned by feminist ecclesiology, is essentially open to the whole of creation. Its commitment to justice includes a concern for the preservation of the whole of creation and a just distribution of limited resources. The church shares in the story of the Triune God and in the interconnectedness of the whole of creation. It is an ecological church.

6. A feminist vision of being church describes the contemporary church as being in need of mysticism, prophecy, poetics, healing and justice, and in creating a space where these are possible anticipates God's eschatological reign as the kin-dom of the divine. The stories of women tell the story of the Triune God as stories of seeking God and finding ways of expressing faith, of uncomfortable and transforming truth-telling as the forth-telling of God's reign. They are stories of creating right relationships of interconnectedness among human beings and with the whole of creation. They are stories of sharing and making women and children visible and of hearing each other into speech and by doing so performing God's being in the world. They are stories of being God's body and being church.

# Bibliography

Allen, Prudence
    1985    *The Concept of Woman: The Aristotelian Revolution 750 BC–AD 1250* (Montreal: Eden Press).

Althaus-Reid, Marcella
    1993    'Walking with Women Serpents', *Ministerial Formation* 62: 31-42.

Benhabib, Seyla
    1987    'The Generalized and the Concrete Other: The Kohlberg-Gilligan Controversy and Feminist Theory', in Seyla Benhabib and Drucilla Cornell (eds.), *Feminism as Critique: Essays on the Politics of Gender in Late-Capitalist Societies* (London: Polity Press): 77-95.

Bonhoeffer, Dietrich
    1967    *Letters and Papers from Prison* (New York: Macmillan, rev. edn).

Børresen, Kari
    1983    'Mary in Catholic Theology', *Concilium* 168: 48-56.

Bouyer, Louis
    1985    *Woman in the Church* (trans. Marilyn Teichert; San Francisco: Ignatius Press).

Bynum, Caroline Walker
    1987    *Holy Feast and Holy Fast: The Religious Significance of Food to Medieval Women* (Berkeley: University of California Press).

Carmody, Denise Lardner
    1995    *Christian Feminist Theology: A Constructive Interpretation* (Oxford: Basil Blackwell).

Chavasse, Claude
    1942    *The Bride of Christ: An Enquiry into the Nuptial Element in Early Christianity* (London: Faber & Faber).

Chaves, Marc
    1997    *Ordaining Women: Culture and Conflict in Religious Organizations* (Cambridge, MA: Harvard University Press).

Chrisman, Miriam U.
    1972    'Women and the Reformation in Strassbourg 1490–1530', in Heinrich Bornkamm *et al.* (eds.), *Three Essays on Women in the Reformation* (Gütersloh: Archiv fuer Reformationsgeschichte): 141-68.

Clark, Elizabeth A.
    1999    'Rewriting Early Christian History', in Gary Macy (ed.), *Theology and the New Histories* (Annual Publication of the College Theological Society, 44; Maryknoll, NY: Orbis Books): 89-111.

Collins, Mary
    1991        'Women in Relation to the Institutional Church' (unpublished paper,
                Leadership Conference of Women Religious 1991 National Assembly,
                Albuquerque, New Mexico).
Daly, Mary
    1967        *The Church and the Second Sex* (New York: Harper & Row).
    1973        *Beyond God the Father: Toward a Philosophy of Women's Liberation* (London:
                The Women's Press).
Davie, Grace
    1994        *Religion in Britain since 1945: Believing without Belonging* (Oxford: Basil
                Blackwell).
D'Costa, Gavin
    2000        *Sexing the Trinity: Gender, Culture and the Divine* (London: SCM Press).
Dorrien, Gary
    1995        *Soul in Society: The Making and Renewal of Social Christianity* (Minneapolis:
                Fortress Press).
Fageol, Suzanne
    1991        'Celebrating Experience', in St Hilda Community (ed.), *Women Included:
                A Book of Services and Prayers* (London: SPCK): 16-26.
Fiorenza, Elisabeth Schüssler
    1982        'Gather Together in My Name… Toward a Christian Feminist Spirituality',
                in Diann Neu and Maria Riley (eds.), *Women Moving Church* (Washington:
                Centre for Concern): 11 and 25.
    1984        *Bread Not Stone: The Challenge of Feminist Biblical Interpretation* (Boston:
                Beacon Press).
    1985        'The Will to Choose or the Reject: Continuing Our Critical Work', in
                Letty M. Russell (ed.), *Feminist Interpretation of the Bible* (Oxford: Basil
                Blackwell): 125-36.
    1993a       *In Memory of Her: A Feminist Theological Reconstruction of Christian Origins*
                (London: SCM Press, 2nd edn).
    1993b       *Discipleship of Equals: A Critical Feminist Ekklesia-logy of Liberation* (London:
                SCM Press).
    1995        *Jesus: Miriam's Child, Sophia's Prophet* (London: SCM Press).
    1997        'Discipleship of Equals: Reality and Vision', in Musimbi R.A. Kanyoro
                (ed.), *In Search of a Round Table: Gender, Theology and Church Leadership*
                (Geneva: WCC): 57-70.
Furlong, Monica
    1991        'A Non-Sexist Community', in St Hilda Community (ed.), *Women Included:
                A Book of Services and Prayers* (London: SPCK): 5-15.
Graef, Hilda
    1963        *Mary: A History of Doctrine and Devotion* (London: Sheed & Ward).
Grey, Mary
    1997a       *Beyond the Dark Night: A Way Forward for the Church* (London: Cassell).
    1997b       *Prophecy and Mysticism: The Heart of the Postmodern Church* (Edinburgh: T. &
                T. Clark).
Gudorf, Christine
    1987        'The Power to Create: Sacraments and Men's Need to Birth', *Horizons*
                14.2: 296-309.

Halkes, Catharina
    1983    'Mary and Women', *Concilium* 168: 66-73.
Hess, Carol Lakey
    1998    'Becoming Mid-wives to Justice: A Feminist Approach to Practical Theology', in Denise M. Ackermann and Riet Bons-Storm (eds.), *Liberating Faith Practices: Feminist Practical Theologies in Context* (Leuven: Peeters): 51-74.
Hildegard of Bingen
    1990    *Scivias* (trans. Mother Columba Hart and Jane Bishop; Classics of Western Spirituality; New York: Paulist Press).
Hudson-Wilkin, Rose
    2001    'Keynote Address at the Women's Ordination Worldwide Conference, Dublin 2001' http.//www.wow2001.org/RHWKey.htm
Hunt, Mary E.
    1989    'Spiral Not Schism: Women-Church as Church', *Religion and Intellectual Life* 7: 82-92.
Irigaray, Luce
    1997    'Equal to Whom?' Translated by Robert L. Mazzola in Graham Ward (ed.), *The Postmodern God: A Reader* (Oxford: Basil Blackwell): 198-213. Original publication: Lucy Irigaray, 'Equal to Whom?' trans. by Robert L. Mazzola, in *differences: A Journal of Feminist Cultural Studies* 1.2 (1989): 59-76.
Isherwood, Lisa, and Elizabeth Stuart
    1998    *Introducing Body Theology* (Sheffield: Sheffield Academic Press).
Jantzen, Grace
    1996    'Disrupting the Sacred: Religion and Gender in the City' (unpublished paper).
Jay, Nancy
    1985    'Sacrifice as Remedy for Having Been Born of Woman', in Constance H. Buchanan, Margaret R. Miles and Clarissa W. Atkinson (eds.), *Immaculate and Powerful: The Female in Sacred Image and Social Reality* (Boston: Beacon Press): 283-309.
    1992    *Throughout Your Generations Forever: Sacrifice, Religion and Paternity* (Chicago: University of Chicago Press).
Johnson, Elizabeth
    1985    'The Marian Tradition and the Reality of Women', *Horizons* 12.1: 116-35.
Jones, Serene
    2000    *Feminist Theory and Christian Theology: Cartographies of Grace* (Minneapolis: Fortress Press).
    2001    'Bounded Openness: Postmodernism, Feminism, and the Church Today', *Interpretation* 55.1: 49-59.
LaCugna, Catherine Mowry
    1991    *God For Us: The Trinity and Christian Life* (San Francisco: Harper).
Maeckelberghe, Els
    1989    '"Mary": Maternal Friend or Virgin Mother', *Concilium* 206: 120-27.
Malone, Mary T.
    2000    *Women and Christianity: The First Thousand Years* (Dublin: Columba Press).
McEwan, Dorothea
    1991    'Summary', in *idem* (ed.), *Women Experiencing Church: A Documentation of Alienation* (Leominster: Gracwing): 247-66.

Miller, Monica Migliorino
    1995        *Sexuality and Authority in the Catholic Church* (Scranton: University of
                Scranton Press).
Moosbach, Carola
    2002        *Traces of Heaven* (ed. Natalie and Giles Watson; London: SPCK).
Morley, Janet, and Hannah Ward
    1995        *Celebrating Women* (London: SPCK).
Morton, Nelle
    1985        *The Journey is Home* (Boston: Beacon Press).
Moser, Michaela
    1995        'Working on Creating Space for Each Other: Towards the First European
                Women's Synod', in Julie Hopkins *et al.* (eds.), *Women Churches: Networking
                and Reflection in the European Context* (Yearbook of the European Society of
                Women in Theological Research; Kampen: Kok Pharos): 100-105.
Mumm, Susan
    1998        *Stolen Daughters, Virgin Mothers: Anglican Sisterhoods in Victorian Britain*
                (London: Cassell).
Petrie, Pat
    1991        'The Church's Control of Sexuality and the Oppression of Women', in
                Dorothea McEwan (ed.), *Women Experiencing Church: A Documentation of
                Alienation* (Leominster: Gracewing): 199-203.
Pierce, Joanne M.
    1999        '"Green Women" and Blood Pollution: Some Medieval Rituals for the
                Churching of Women after Childbirth', *Studia Liturgica* 29: 191-215.
Plaskow, Judith
    1980        *Sex, Sin and Grace: Women's Experiences in the Theologies of Reinhold Niebuhr
                and Paul Tillich* (Washington: University of America Press).
Raphael, Melissa
    1996        *Thealogy and Embodiment: The Post-Patriarchal Reconstruction of Female Sacrality*
                (Sheffield: Sheffield Academic Press).
Rasolondraibe, Péri
    1997        'Foreword: Making a Difference', in Musimbi R.A. Kanyoro (ed.), *In
                Search of a Round Table: Gender, Theology and Church Leadership* (Geneva:
                WCC): vii-viii.
Riley, Maria, and Diann Neu (eds.)
    1982        *Women Moving Church* (Washington: Centre for Concern).
Roll, Susan K.
    2000        'Baptism: New Thinking from Women-identified Perspectives', *Questions
                Liturgiques/Studies in Liturgy* 81/3-4: 302-16.
    2002        'The Old Rite of the Churching of Women After Childbirth', in Anne-
                Marie Korte *et al.* (eds.), *Blood, Purity and Impurity* (Religion and Discourse
                series; Edinburgh: Peter Lang, in press).
Ross, Susan A.
    1989        '"Then Honor God in Your Body" (1. Cor. 6.20): Feminist and
                Sacramental Theology on the Body', *Horizons* 16.1: 7-27.
    1993        'God's Embodiment and Women: Sacraments', in Catherine Mowry
                LaCugna (ed.), *Freeing Theology: The Essentials of Theology in Feminist
                Perspective* (San Francisco: Harper): 185-209.

1995        'Extravagant Affections: Women's Sexuality and Theological Anthropology', in Ann O'Hara Graff (ed.), *In the Embrace of God: Feminist Approaches to Theological Anthropology* (Maryknoll, NY: Orbis Books): 105-121.

1998        *Extravagant Affections: Feminist Perspectives on Sacramental Theology* (New York: Continuum).

Ruether, Rosemary Radford

1975        *New Woman, New Earth: Sexist Ideologies and Human Liberation* (Boston: Seabury Press).

1979        *Mary: The Feminine Face of the Church* (London: SCM Press).

1983        *Sexism and God-Talk: Toward a Feminist Theology* (Boston: Beacon Press).

1985        'Feminist Interpretation: A Method of Correlation', in Letty Russell (ed.), *Feminist Interpretation of the Bible* (Oxford: Basil Blackwell): 111-24.

1986a      Women-Church: Emerging Feminist Liturgical Communities', in Norbert Greinacher and Norbert Mette (eds.), *Popular Religion* (Edinburgh: T. & T. Clark): 52-59.

1986b      'Differing Views of the Church', in Madonna Kolbenschlag (ed.), *Authority, Community and Conflict* (Kansas: Sheed & Ward): 96-107.

1987        'The Call of Women in the Church', in Virginia Ramey Mollenkott (ed.), *Women of Faith in Dialogue* (New York: Crossroad): 77-88.

1988        *Women-Church: Theology and Praxis of Feminist Liturgical Communities* (San Francisco: Harper & Row).

1993a      'The Women-Church Movement in Contemporary Christianity', in Catherine Wessinger (ed.), *Women's Leadership in Marginal Religions: Explorations Outside the Mainstream* (Urbana, IL: University of Illinois Press): 196-210.

1993b      *Gaia and God: An Ecofeminist Theology of Earth Healing* (London: SCM Press).

1995        'Being a Catholic Feminist at the End of the Twentieth Century', *Feminist Theology* 10: 9-20.

1996        'Women-Church: An American Catholic Feminist Movement' (unpublished paper).

Scheffczyk, Leo

1988        'Mary as a Model of Catholic Faith', in Helmut Moll (ed.), *The Church and Women: A Compendium* (San Francisco: Ignatius Press): 83-102.

Schroeder, Joy A.

1991        'Toward a Feminist Eucharistic Theology and Piety', *Dialog* 30.3: 221-26.

Semmelroth, Otto

1963        *Mary, Archetype of the Church* (trans. Maria von Eroes and John Devlin; Dublin: Gill and Son).

Society of Friends

1994        *Quaker Faith and Practice: The Book of Christian Discipline of the Yearly Meeting of the Religious Society of Friends (Quakers) in Britain* (Society of Friends).

Stancliffe, David

1998        'This is our Story. This is our Song. Hosannah in the Highest', *Church Times* (27 February): 12.

Walker, Andrew

1985        *Restoring the Kingdom: The Radical Christianity of the House Church Movement* (London: Hodder & Stoughton).

Weedon, Chris
    1987          *Feminist Praxis and Poststructuralist Theory* (Oxford: Basil Blackwell).
Wetherilt, Ann Kirkus
    1994          *That They Be Many: Voices of Women, Echoes of God* (New York: Continuum).
Wijngaards, John
    2001          'Discerning the Spirit's New Creation' (Paper presented at the First
                Women's Ordination Worldwide Conference, Dublin 2001) http.//www.
                wow2001.org/jwpaper.htm
Winter, M.T., Admir Lumis and Allison Stokes (eds.)
    1994          *Defecting in Place: Women Claiming Responsibility for their own Spiritual Lives*
                (New York: Crossroad).
Young, Iris Marion
    1990a         *Justice and the Politics of Difference* (Princeton, NJ: Princeton University
                Press).
    1990b         'The Ideal of Community and the Politics of Justice', in Linda Nicholson
                (ed.), *Feminism/Postmodernism* (New York: Routledge): 300-323.
Young, Pamela Dickey
    2000          *Re-creating the Church: Communities of Eros* (Harrisburgh: Trinity Press
                International).
Zikmund, Barbara Brown
    1986          'Winning Ordination for Women in Mainstream Protestant Churches', in
                Rosemary Radford Ruether and Rosemary Skinner Keller (eds.), *Women
                and Religion in America*. III. *1900–1968* (San Francisco: Harper & Row):
                339-83.
Zizioulas, John D.
    1985          *Being as Communion: Studies in Personhood and the Church* (London: Darton,
                Longman & Todd).

# Index of Authors

# Other books in the
## *Introductions in Feminist Theology* series

*Introducing African Women's Theology*
Mercy Amba Oduyoye

Mercy Amba Oduyoye describes the context and methodology of Christian theology by Africans in the past two decades, offering brief descriptions and sample treatments of theological issues such as creation, Christology, ecclesiology, and eschatology. The daily spiritual life of African Christian women is evident as the reader is led to the sources of African women's Christian theology. This book reflects how African culture and its multi-religious context has influenced women's selection of theological issues.
ISBN 1-84127-143-8
Paper, 136 pages
£12.95

*Introducing Asian Feminist Theology*
Kwok Pui-Lan

The book introduces the history, critical issues, and direction of feminist theology as a grass roots movement in Asia. Kwok Pui-Lan takes care to highlight the diversity of this broad movement, noting that not all women theologians in Asia embrace feminism. Amid a diverse range of sociopolitical, religiocultural, postcultural, and postcolonial contexts, this book lifts up the diversity of voices and ways of doing feminist theology while attending to women's experiences, how the Bible is interpreted, and the ways that Asian religious traditions are appropriated. It searches out a passionate, life-affirming spirituality through feminine images of God, new metaphors for Christ, and a reformulation of sin and redemption.
ISBN 1-84127-066-0
Paper, 136 pages
£12.95

*Introducing Body Theology*
Lisa Isherwood and Elizabeth Stuart

Because Christianity asserts that God was incarnated in human form, one might expect that its theologies would be body affirming. Yet for women (and indeed also for gay men) the body has been the site for oppression. *Introducing Body Theology* offers a body-centered theology that discusses cosmology, ecology, ethics, immortality, and sexuality, in a concise introduction that proposes and encourages a positive theology of the body.
ISBN 1-85075-995-2
Paper, 168 pages
£12.95


*Introducing Feminist Images of God*
Mary Grey

Mary Grey presents recent thinking reflecting early attempts to move beyond restrictive God language, opening up the possibilities of more inclusive ways of praying. The rich experiences of God, distinctive and diverse, are seen through the eyes of many different cultures and the women who struggle for justice. Using the figure of Sophia Wisdom as an example, Grey shows that there are many still-unplumbed images of God to discover.
ISBN 1-84127-160-8
Paper, 136 pages
£12.95


*Introducing a Practical Feminist Theology of Worship*
Janet Wootton

Only three great women-songs are retained in the Bible: Deborah's song for ordinary people, Hannah's song of triumph, and Mary's song at meeting her cousin Elizabeth. Many others, such as Miriam's song, are truncated or over-shadowed by male triumphs. *Introducing a Practical Feminist Theology of Worship* begins by revealing how women have been 'whispering liturgy.' It then explores female images of God, discusses how worship spaces function, and

offers practical suggestions for how women can use words and movements to construct authentic forms of worship.
ISBN 1-84127-067-9
Paper, 148 pages
£12.95


*Introducing Redemption in Christian Feminism*
Rosemary R. Ruether

*Introducing Redemption in Christian Feminism* explores the dichotomy between two patterns of thinking found in Christianity: the redemption of Christ being applied to all without regard to gender, and the exclusion of women from leadership because women were created subordinate to men and because women were more culpable for sin. After examining these two patterns, Ruether examines some key theological themes: Christology, the self, the cross, and eschatology.
ISBN 1-85075-888-3
Paper, 136 pages
£12.95


*Introducing Thealogy: Discourse on the Goddess*
Melissa Raphael

*Introducing Thealogy* provides an accessible but critical introduction to the relationship of religion, theo/alogy, and gender, especially as these concepts unfold in the revival of Goddess religion among feminists in Europe, North America, and Australasia. Raphael focuses on the boundaries of that broad movement, what is meant by the Goddess, theology in history and ethics, the political implications of the movement, and how it relates to feminist witchcraft.
ISBN 1-85075-975-8
Paper, 184 pages
£12.95

*Introducing Feminist Christologies*
Lisa Isherwood

In this imaginative book, Lisa Isherwood challenges the oppressive model of
an all-powerful God and highlights feminist interpretations of Christ across
the globe. She attempts to chart a course from questioning the relevance of a
male savior to women—to the many faces of Christ that have emerged from
the lives of women (Jesus as lover, friend, or shaman, amongst other things)—
to a place of reflection about the nature of Christological thinking in the
twenty-first century.
ISBN 1-84127-250-7
Paper, 144 pages
£14.99